Village Bread, Olive Oil and a Grandmother's Blessings

First published in November 2011
Copyright - Elena Demetriou 2011

ISBN: 1456346970
ISBN-13: 9781456346973

Designed by Paperdrops
Printed by Lithostar

About the author

A Greek-Cypriot born in a tiny village called Lysos, on the Mediterranean island of Cyprus, Elena Demetriou immigrated to South Africa with her parents when she was 6 years old. After adapting to life in a suburb of Johannesburg and completing her school education, she obtained a degree in dental surgery. Elena considers herself to be a philomath (a lover of learning) and besides running a busy dental practise she also has a great passion for: reading and writing, cooking and eating home-made food, spending time with her extra large family, traveling and sharing her Greek-Cypriot culture with the world. Elena Demetriou won second prize at the Cyprus South African business woman of the year event which was held at the Elea golf estate in Paphos on the 25th May 2012.

I dedicate this book to my selfless grandparents, to Savvaki, Charouli, Didi and Natalia, to my husband, to Susanna my proof reader, to my friends around the globe, and to all the members of my dramatic but loving Greek-Cypriot family! I would like to thank Nektarios Photography, my editors, publishing team, printing house and last but not least, my friend Elpitha for all her valuable help with my computer.

The above photo is one of my favorites; it shows my mother's side of the family, standing in an organized state of chaos, at my sister Dora's wedding.

Introduction

There are three things that you should find in every Greek-Cypriot home: fresh village bread, virgin olive oil, and at least one faithful *yiayia* [grandmother] who is always praying and giving out her blessings. I wish that every child in this world could grow up with these three things. I am grateful for my family and proud of my Greek-Cypriot heritage, and I would like to share a part of my life with the world, even though I am not a victim of great suffering, a celebrity, or a politician. I decided to write about the times I would like to remember when I am old—just in case I end up with Alzheimer's disease like my *yiayia* Haritou (God forbid).

Food is mentioned often throughout this book because I am one of the few women I know who has eaten almost everything, and because food has filled my mind (and my expanded stomach) with pleasant, everlasting memories. May all the children of Cyprus cherish and preserve our traditions.

Chapter 1:

It All Started
with a Wedding Ceremony

It was the twenty-fifth of September in 1977, and the warm air was filled with the bustle and nervous excitement of the relatives. Two young strangers from two different villages would be joined together in marriage. My twenty-year-old mother wore a borrowed, white satin dress with floral trimmings, and her wavy, auburn hair was combed by her *koumera* [maid of honor]. My father's rough, chiseled face was shaved gently by his *koumbaro* [best man] with a straight razor, in the yard under the watchful eyes of some guests. My father looks very serious in the photo below; it was probably the sensation of the cold, sharp razor against his throat. (I will assume that back then there was no such thing as pre-wedding jitters.)

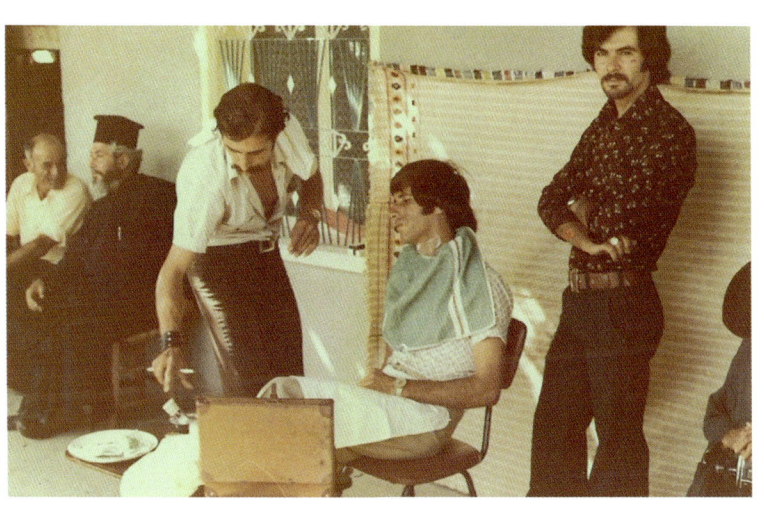

The wedding was held in a tiny village called Lysos, on the beautiful island of Cyprus. For the perplexed readers that have never heard of Cyprus, you really need to get out more; you should find a patriotic Cypriot under every 'rock', or else you can search for it on Google's maps. It is the third largest island found in the Mediterranean Sea and is situated north of Israel, to the east of the Greek island of Crete, south of Turkey, and to the west of Syria.

In Cyprus every ceremony begins and ends with an abundance of food, so a few days before the wedding, the close relatives prepared the wheat. The wheat grain (without the sheath) was washed at the village fountain and ground by an old stone mill with a long wooden handle that was pushed by three or four people. The wheat grain was then used to make an immense amount of the favorite wedding food-*resi* [slow-cooked wheat grain with goat's meat, lemon juice, salt, and pepper]; it looks a bit like mushy porridge.

The macho male relatives slaughtered and prepared a dozen lambs. On the day of the wedding the meat would be cut into pieces, sprinkled with salt, oregano, and lemon, wrapped in foil, and slow cooked for many hours in sealed, outdoor stone ovens. (Meat cooked in this way melts in the mouth.) This traditional wedding dish is called *kleftiko*. *Kleftiko* comes from the Greek word for thief, and it's used for this dish because during the wars, hungry rebels that were in hiding in the mountains stole goats and lambs from the villagers and cooked the meat for many hours underground.

The female relatives baked many loaves of sesame coated village bread, huge trays of golden potatoes, and *pasticho* [macaroni with minced pork meat covered with béchamel sauce]. They had to feed and satisfy over a thousand hungry guests.

Just before the church service, my parents' double bed mattress, adorned with a patterned, handmade bedspread, was laid outside. Four maiden virgins sewed crosses with red ribbons in the corners, and then a baby boy was rolled onto the mattress so that the wedding couple would be blessed with fertility. The relatives threw money on a handkerchief that was placed on top of the mattress as a symbol of good luck, which was meant to bring money to the couple.

Throughout the ceremony, a live band played traditional wedding songs with a Cypriot violin and a Greek *bouzouki*. Cypriot wedding songs have the same effect as chopping onions, as they extract the tears of all the female relatives. Wedding days are very sad for the mother and daughter, since the daughter has to leave her parents and spend the rest of her life with her husband. In Cyprus, before the church service, the parents take turns wrapping a red handkerchief around the couple's waists three times, which represents the Holy Trinity. The parents and grandparents give their blessings and burn incense. After a one-hour church service and the priest's blessing, the dancing and feasting begin.

My mother and father danced to the rhythm of the wedding songs that were played by a live orchestra. The traditional Cypriot wedding dance is nothing like the passionate dance of salsa; the couple stands a meter away from each other and moves back and forth in short, timid steps. The relatives and guests took turns pinning banknotes (at that time, Cypriot pounds or *lires*) to the couple's clothing, until long chains of *lires* united them together. The parents saved up their most valuable *lires* to pin to the couple's garments, so as not to feel shamed in front of the scrutinizing eyes of the new in-laws. That was probably the last time my conservative father boogied on a dance floor with my mother.

To this day, at Cypriot weddings the guests give money instead of gifts. There is a big, decorated money box at the entrance of the reception, where the couple and their parents stand for hours to greet their guests, who usually arrive late and in driblets. After the handshakes, gentle kisses on both cheeks, and many congratulations, the couple is handed a little white envelope with the guest's name written boldly on the exterior; the envelope is dropped into the slotted box. Money is appreciated more than a kettle or a toaster because it contributes to the down payment on a new home. The day after the wedding, instead of rushing off to a romantic honeymoon, Cypriot couples are usually busy opening envelopes, counting money, and making notes on who gave what. All the money received is basically borrowed, because when the guest or the guest's son or daughter gets married, the couple will be expected to give the same amount of money as a gift at that wedding.

When my sister and her husband opened their envelopes the day after their wedding, they found four envelopes were empty and one contained a lottery ticket; those envelopes probably came from some unscrupulous wedding crashers. There can be up to four thousand people at some Cypriot weddings, since the couple's parents invite all the members of their extended families, all the neighbors from their village, as well as the inhabitants of the neighboring villages. The couple usually doesn't recognize half the guests. The more people the parents invite, the more money their children will make at their wedding. The guests usually eat very well; they definitely get their money's worth, and probably two days of indigestion. The men drink many bottles of Cypriot beer and as many shots of *zivania* as they can handle. *Zivania* is a strong, clear alcoholic spirit made from grapes and is stronger than vodka. It is so strong that my grannies would rub it onto their painful knee joints and it instantly relieved their pain. (It is also great for cleaning windows.) The women receive their **bonbonieres** [wedding gifts that are wrapped with a doily containing an even number of almond sweets], and all the guests are given sweet *lokoumia* [wedding biscuits that are stuffed with almonds or pistachio nuts and sprinkled with confectioner's sugar, which powders your face when you take a bite]. A wedding is not complete without the *lokoumia*. My mother's honorable father gave them a gift of two thousand Cypriot pounds that he had saved for his eldest daughter. My parents used the money to buy an old house up on a hill in my father's village of Lysos. In the days when houses were still cheap, it was the custom for Cypriot parents to marry off their daughters and buy them a house. Sons were educated or taught a trade so that they could support their new family. In my parent's case, their new family was soon to come.

Chapter 2:

My Sweet Childhood in Little Cyprus

Nine months after my parents were married, I was born on their blessed double-bed mattress in the village of Lysos. The reason I was born at home in the "modern" year of 1978 was because my mother had early labor pains, and there was not enough time for my panic-stricken father to drive her to the city hospital. Thanks to God and Yianoulla, the confident village midwife, my mother safely delivered a healthy baby—me! My mother should have known there and then that I was not going to be a placid child...

There is no better place for a curious child to grow up than in a village surrounded by nature. I was very adventurous and perhaps spoiled, as Cypriot firstborns usually are. I always got my way. I remember my childhood in vivid detail. I hated being indoors, and I often wandered off into the neighboring fields around our house to play. I picked wild flowers like yellow daisies, pink anemones, and blood-red poppies, and I made vases for my flowers out of empty, rusted tin cans that I found abandoned in the fields.

I loved to walk to the house of my kind, deeply wrinkled great-granny, Angelou. She was my father's grandmother, and she lived down the hill, just a few minutes from our house. She was toothless, her chin jutted out, and her shortened spine was so hunched over that the hunchback of Notre Dame would have been envious. I remember playing with the skin on her hands; it was very elastic and soft when I pinched and pulled it upward. *Yiayia* Angelou always wore black from her head scarf to her worn leather shoes (she was a widow and that was the tradition), and she always held a crooked, wooden walking stick. I gave her my flower gifts, and in return she smiled and said, "*Tin efchin mou na xeis*" ["You have my blessing"].

She would pour me some fragrant *triantafilo* [red rose syrup] with milk, and on a miniature glass plate she placed my favorite Cypriot sweet, *karithaki*, which is a whole walnut that has been preserved in syrup and cloves; it looks like a small, black ball. I would often get in trouble from my mother for dripping syrup on my dresses. Some days, she let me eat some of her canned condensed milk with a teaspoon. Who can blame me for having such a sweet tooth today?

My gentle great-grandmother was about 105 years old when she passed away. (Her grandchildren lost track of her exact age after she passed a century.) Up until her hundredth year, she was strong enough to make her own Greek coffee and prepare her own simple meals. When she could no longer walk long distances, her son-in-law cut a hole in the center of an old village chair, put a bucket underneath the hole, and that became Granny Angelou's toilet.

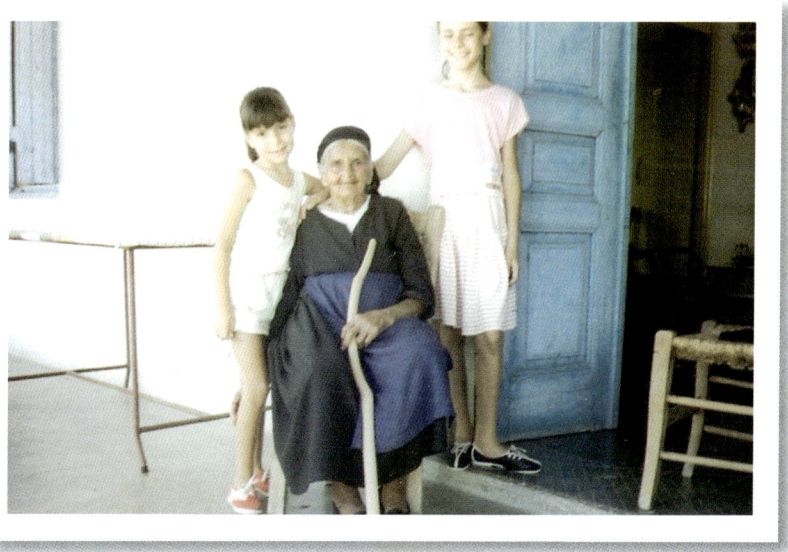

In those days everyone in the village was self-sufficient. There were no big supermarkets, only a local *kafenio* [coffee shop] that sold a few basic necessities. The *kafenio* was also the meeting place of silver-haired men that would gather to debate politics and slurp Greek coffee from small porcelain cups. Somehow, like the rest of the villagers, we had everything we needed.

My father tended many citrus and olive trees, and every year the trees rewarded him with their fruits. As far back as I can remember, we had a bowl of olives on our kitchen table. There were green olives that were cracked open by my mother with a round stone and served with lemon, olive oil, garlic, and wild oregano. There were brown, wrinkled olives that tasted salty and bitter, and there were black, shiny smooth olives that were preserved in vinegar and tasted sweet. I went to the village olive mill with my father and his many boxes of handpicked olives. I watched as the olives were pressed and turned into earthy-smelling, golden-green olive oil. The old man that ran the olive press would grill a few slices of village bread over a gas stove, and when the olive oil was ready, he would pour some on a plate; then he added lemon, salt, and wild oregano. He would offer me a piece of toast that was dunked in the tasty mixture. I crunched away at my toast until the olive oil was dripping down my chin.

We had our own vegetable garden, and we kept a few farm animals in an abandoned ruin of a house that was in the field behind our house. I fed our muddy pig scraps of homegrown pumpkin or vegetable peels that my mother had discarded, and I loved to listen to him squeal and grunt while he ate. Like an eager detective, I searched for eggs in the chicken pen; I watched with fascination as my mother skinned and dissected our gray rabbits when they were fat enough for stew. The rabbit was slow cooked with plenty of onions, a bay leaf, salt, a drop of vinegar, and some red wine. (We call this dish *stifadho*.) I watched my mother pluck the feathers off our plump white chickens when it was their turn to become lunch. She often made my favorite dish—chicken pieces stewed with *kolokassi*, a locally grown fat, brown root that resembles the sweet potato. *Kolokassi* is peeled, dried with a kitchen towel, and fried in olive oil until golden and then cooked slowly with wine and lemon juice—it is a popular Cypriot dish.

After it rained, I would rush outside to look for the biggest snails that had crawled out from their hiding places. We put them in a perforated bucket and fed them flour for a few days to clean out their intestines.

My mother boiled the snails three times, draining the water each time until all the yucky slime was gone, then she served them in their shells. We used a toothpick to get the snail out of its shell and pulled off the mucky bit at the end, which was not eaten. We dipped the edible part of the snail into a mixture of olive oil, salt, and red wine vinegar. The leftover snails were pickled in a jar for later. Nothing was thrown away.

My sisters and I were taught to eat everything from a young age. There were no fussy eaters at our table. If our mother boiled a lamb's head, we had no choice but to eat the lamb's head. The brain was actually the best part, and I remember my father scooping it out with a spoon and feeding us. He also taught us to suck the marrow out of our bones. There were no restaurants or takeout joints in the village; if you didn't eat what your mother prepared, you would have starved.

In the wintertime, we walked to the nearby pine forest to look for the sweet, meaty-tasting, wild red mushrooms that were hidden under a few tall pine trees. My father had a gift for remembering exactly which trees were hiding the biggest mushrooms, and of course which mushrooms to avoid if they were poisonous. He grilled them over our fireplace and served them with olive oil, salt, and fresh lemon juice. I will never understand people's fuss over expensive truffles; they are tasteless compared to wild red mushrooms, and the red mushrooms are free if you know where to look.

I hiked in the rocky hills with my mother, and I watched her cut bunches of *rigani* [fragrant wild oregano], mountain tea, thorny thyme bushes, *horta* [wild edible green plants that were boiled], and *kapari* [wild caper leaves, which were pickled]. My mother would point out the wild plants that were edible and the ones that were poisonous. During our hikes I rescued prickly hedgehogs from the sandy roads because I was afraid they would be squashed by passing tractors.

My father's mom, *Yiayia* Haritou, lived next door to her aged mother, my great-granny Angelou, and she took care of her mother with the little patience that was left in her bones. *Yiayia* Haritou was one of the tidiest women in her village, and she had an amusing, dry sense of humor. She had a hint of a moustache because, in those days, hair removal was not a priority, and she pricked my cheeks every time she bent over to kiss me. In Cyprus, children, especially babies with chubby cheeks, are smothered with kisses by all their close relatives. Our granny took us for short rides in her yard on her weary-looking donkey.

I remember sitting on the cool doorstep of *Yiayia* Haritou's house and watching her prepare the **shoushouko**, a Cypriot treat that looks like a long sausage and is made from grape juice, flour, and fragrant water. My granny strung a lot of almonds together, dipped them into the grape juice mixture, and hung them up on her washing line to drip dry. This was repeated seven times until the **shoushouko** was nice and thick. Because it preserved well, **shoushouko** was eaten all through the year, and many women had it in their pantry to offer unexpected guests.

When she'd finished preparing the *shoushouko*, *Yiayia* Haritou would make the *palouze*. To do this, she boiled the leftover grape juice in a large cauldron over a fire; as it cooked, she threw in a type of white sand and, with a big spoon, skimmed the froth that formed on top. The sand settled at the bottom and made the grape juice sweeter by regulating the acidity. The grape mixture was strained and mixed with flour until it became a thick, caramel-colored jelly. The jelly was put into bowls and sprinkled with crushed walnuts.

She also made the best Cypriot *glyka tou koutaliou* [spoon sweets], which are different types of raw fruits or vegetables, walnuts, and citrus fruit peels, which are boiled with a lot of sugar and fragrant spices like cinnamon and cloves, and then stored in glass jars. Those were the sweets I ate as a child. Sadly, *Yiayia* Haritou passed away while I was writing this book. She was 93 years old and unfortunately she suffered from Alzheimer's disease the last five years of her life, but I will always remember the strong, independent woman that she was when I was a child.

Occasionally I stayed over at the house of my *Yiayia* Theodora, who is my maternal grandmother. Her house is in the neighboring village of Steni, which is a ten-minute drive away from Lysos. I was her first grandchild and, to this day, she spoils me with words of praise and special blessings. I have never heard one bad word escape from *Yiayia* Theodora's mouth. When the children or adults in our family had arguments, she would tell us to forgive and love each other, without taking sides. I have never heard her complain about her burdensome life; she is always praising and thanking God. I believe that she is one of my few connections to God, and I envy her unwavering faith. When I look into her chestnut eyes, I sense an aura of integrity, as if I am staring into the soul of a nun, and I believe that as long as she is praying for us to be healthy and safe, we have nothing to fear.

In *Yiayia* Theodora's front yard, there was a swing made out of a thick rope and a wooden plank that hung from a giant carob tree. (Carob trees are evergreen trees and are found all over Cyprus.) As I swung back and forth, I watched my shadow fly over a pond that was the home to a school of tiny black fish. There was a shaggy jasmine tree outside my granny's front door, and when the white flowers were in bloom, it filled the air with its heavenly scent. One of the neighbors that drank her morning coffee with my granny would clip a few sprigs of jasmine and hide them in her petticoat pocket. The front yard was also cluttered with many tin pots of sweet-smelling, leafy green basil.

During the hot summers, *Yiayia* Theodora let me sleep in the backyard with her, under the stars, in an old squeaky bed. As I lay in bed, I watched the black fruit bats fly above the sleeping lemon tree and snuggled close to her for safety, praying hard for the bats not to land on us. I had never seen a bat before until one flew through an open window into my granny's bedroom and landed behind her bed. I thought that it was a swallow, but when I went closer to pick it up, I was greeted by a beastly looking mouse with wings and pointed fangs.

Just before the sunrise, when my granny's psycho rooster emitted his first wake-up call, she would get up, grab her buckets, and head for her goats. Naturally, I followed. I watched my granny milk the swollen teats of the female goats. She made it look easy, but when I tried, I could not squeeze out a single drop. I remember making conversation with brown, smooth-haired goats and white, fluffy goats. I fed them black carobs from the carob tree, and I watched their jaws move side to side as they chewed. (A carob is the black pod of the carob tree; in Cyprus it is used to make naturally sweet syrup that is exported and called the black gold by the locals). When my granny's buckets were heavy with goat's milk, she carried them into her tiny kitchen and went to work making different kinds of milk products.

My granny made various types of Cypriot cheese. She made *halloumi*, a salty, white, smooth cheese fragranced with mint that is great for grilling, and *anari*, which looks like cottage cheese and is served warm with sweet carob syrup. She also made a salty version of the *anari* cheese, which was compressed and strained in little basket holders, dried, and later grated over pasta. She also made sour-smelling, smooth yoghurt and *trahana*, which is a thick mixture of wheat grain and sour milk that is cut into small pieces and dried in the sun; once dry, it is boiled in chicken stock to make a soup which is a favorite in the winter. I remember my granny climbing to the flat roof of her little house to lay out many sheets of *trahana* to dry.

All the Cypriot women I know are wonderful cooks and gracious hostesses. Any guest is warmly welcomed to their homes and served the best treat they have in their pantry or fridge. Most Cypriot grandmothers are very selfless; they take care of the grandchildren when the parents are at work, and they cook for the whole family. They cook with love and patience to please their husband, children or grandchildren. Growing up, I remember all my female relatives spending most of their time in the kitchen. That is where my passion for homemade food began. The kitchen was also a great place for female bonding and catching up on the latest gossip.

I recently traveled to a mountain village in Limassol and I snapped a photo of a friendly granny standing outside her home. Later that evening, while I was studying my pictures, I discovered that the word 'ROCK' is imprinted on her blouse; she only speaks Greek and probably has no idea. Cypriot grannies 'ROCK' and they are also the rock that keeps the family together.

Our grannies may have grown up in poverty, and during a time of war, but I am pretty sure that no Cypriot child ever died of hunger. Back then, a meal could consist of some olives, a tomato, a piece of *halloumi*, and maybe some figs or grapes when they were in season. During the week they ate wild edible plants, salads, vegetables, lentils, different types of beans, and goat's milk products. On weekends and special holidays, they slaughtered their farm animals and ate meat. Village bread was a key component of every meal because it helped to fill up the hungry hole of the stomach. Even though they ate a lot of bread, they stayed slim. They worked off the calories by walking to and from their fields and from the physical labor involved in farming the land. Village bread was the first solid that was given to babies when they started to teethe. As a child I was always told to eat all my bread so that I could get full—which explains my current inability to follow a carbohydrate-free diet. If Mr. Atkins lived in Cyprus, he would never be able to stick to his famous diet. Village bread is too good to resist.

Yiayia Theodora had an old stone oven in her backyard. Once a week she baked seven loaves of bread for the days to come. There is nothing better in this world than a slice of warm village bread straight out of a stone oven, spread with a generous amount of homemade *mosfilo* jam, which is made from a small, seedy, yellow berry that grows on a tree in the fields of Cyprus. Every Sunday, after the church service, my granny prepared one of her chickens or rabbits and made delicious *psito* [roast] with homegrown potatoes in her stone oven. We loved to dip our bread in the tasty, leftover fatty juices at the bottom of the pan. There is something about a stone oven that makes everything taste better. Yes, I was a blessed child.

In Cyprus, children are considered a great blessing. The older generation of Cypriots had this manic belief that their main purposes in life were, first, to have children, and, second, to help their children as much as possible until the day they died. Offspring were a guarantee that they would have someone to take care of them when they could no longer take care of themselves. The more children they had, the less likely that they would land in an old-age home. Because the cost of living has risen, modern Cypriot couples are thinking twice before having babies. A few years ago, in order to increase the local population, the government resorted to "bribery"—the more children one had, the more money the government sent in the post (mail). Cypriots pity any woman over the age of twenty-five who is single or childless, so matchmaking is the favorite pastime of married female relatives. (My mother is still trying to find a suitable husband for her fifty-five-year-old, shy, virgin cousin.)

Both my grannies had five children each, but since there was no television back then, it was not uncommon to have up to fourteen children. My maternal grandparents were so poor that my mother and her four siblings shared two beds until they were teenagers. *Thea* [Aunt] Maria, my mother's youngest sister, remembers sleeping in a room that had a mountain of wheat grains stacked to the roof. As a child, she ran up the hill of grain to play. The poor villagers in the past shared their homes with their food supplies, and a few even shared their homes with their goats.

Most of the men who lived in the village were farmers. Every morning they traveled miles by foot or donkey to their fields; their wives and young children made the journey with them. My grandmother Theodora told me that while she sat on the donkey on the way to the fields, she kept herself busy with needlework. She eventually made each of her children a beautiful bedspread, which she gave them on their wedding day.

The devoted farmers' wives spent many hours under the harsh Cypriot sun. In those days, there were no sun creams or sunglasses, and it was not fashionable for village women to wear hats. Unfortunately, *Yiayia* Theodora ended up with skin cancer later on in her life. My granny also told me about a few pregnant women who unexpectedly gave birth while working in the fields. In my granny's village the women sowed seeds, collected various crops like tobacco, potatoes, wheat, almonds, walnuts, olives, vegetables and fruit, and also took care of the farm animals.

In addition to their farm chores, the women were responsible for all the laborious house chores and the children's needs. It was their duty to take care of their aged parents and any lonely, elderly relatives who had no children of their own. The women made their family's clothing, bedding, and carpets. My granny grew her own cotton and even kept silkworms and used the yellow cocoons to make silk sheets. When my granny was young there was no running water in the homes, so water was fetched from the local well in large clay vessels. The family's dirty laundry had to be taken down to the river to be scrubbed by hand. (I thank the man that invented the washing machine.) Once a week, water was boiled over a fire and then used to bathe all the children. Back then, the toilets in the village were circular holes dug into the floor, surrounded by a wooden cubicle, which was built a few meters away from the main house. *Thea* Maria told me that when she was young, she dropped one of her shoes by mistake in the hole; she'd just made her "number two" and was too disgusted to fish it out, even though she only owned two pairs of shoes. She also told me that they tore pages out of their old schoolbooks and used them as toilet paper, and that they used pieces of cloth as sanitary pads. We are so spoiled today that we take everything for granted.

My grandfathers were both hardworking, down-to-earth men. My paternal *pappou* [grandfather], Omeros, sailed to America with his brothers when he was just a teenager. He worked for twenty years in a Brooklyn restaurant that, according to my uncle, was owned by the Italian mafia, but he was homesick and miserable because he was not treated very well. In his late thirties, he left America and returned to Cyprus with a few hundred dollars in his pocket (which was considered a lot in those days). He married my grandmother Haritou, who was ten years younger than him and settled in his village of Lysos. He had a proud posture, neatly combed hair, and a Roman-looking nose. *Pappou* Omeros was one of the few men in the village who spoke English. He ran a small coffee shop and farmed a few pieces of land that he inherited from his wife's family. My meticulous grandfather wanted everything clean, tidy, and its place—a trait inherited by all of his children and most of his grandchildren.

When my father was a child, he watched as the English soldiers vandalized their coffee shop during the English occupation and forced his father to act as their translator. After the many hardships they faced in the village, my father's parents became short tempered with their children. My paternal grandfather never sent his children to high school because he needed the extra help in the fields. My *theo* [uncle] Savvas (my father's older brother) told me he was overwhelmed with disappointment when his father stopped him from boarding the school bus that collected the kids from the village and took them to the high school in the town.

I have very few memories of *Pappou* Omeros. I remember him sitting on a village chair, smoking his pipe and carving a flute out of a bamboo stick. I also remember him arguing with his wife on a regular basis. They were both strong characters and clashed often. *Yiayia* Haritou would whisper humorous, sarcastic remarks behind his back. (When I was a child I never understood why couples argued, but now that I am married, it is as clear as a cloudless sky.) Unfortunately, *Pappou* Omeros passed away when I was in primary school, and I never had the opportunity to ask him about his life in America or to bond with him as a grandchild.

Growing up I spent more time with my maternal grandfather, *Pappou* Savvas. He had a hunched upper spine (which comes with age), had only a bit of white hair at the back of his crown and above his ears, and he had a thick, white moustache. I can still picture him sitting cross-legged on his hand-woven chair in his tiny kitchen. He enjoyed talking to his wife while she prepared the daily meals. He loved my granny very much and even wrote her love letters in his old age. He earned my granny's respect because he was honest, hardworking, and patient with her and their children. She fried his favorite vegetables, like zucchini with chili peppers or wild asparagus and horta with eggs and *halloumi*. She made his beloved olive bread from scratch. *Pappou* Savvas preferred his eggs fried in olive oil with salt and a squeeze of lemon; occasionally I eat my eggs this way and they are delicious. He never ate pork and he never slaughtered any of his farm animals because he was too squeamish; my grandmother had to do that nasty work, but she didn't mind because they each had their own chores.

Pappou Savvas adored all his grandchildren, and he was a great storyteller. Wide-eyed, we hung on to his every word, and when he was done, we begged for more. I remember a story about a cave in Steni village that collapsed after a sudden storm and killed a thief who was hiding inside. The thief was in hiding because he had stolen the golden eyes from the icon of the Virgin Mary from the Church of the Panayia, which is found on top of a hill in Steni. My grandfather told us many stories about the Virgin Mary, the saints, and the various miracles they performed in the village.

On Christmas Eve, he told us stories about the *kalikantzari*. These are ugly, gremlin like creatures that supposedly come to earth during Christmas time and create all sorts of mischief. We were told to throw *loukanika* [Cypriot pork sausages] on the roof so that these creatures would have something to eat and leave us alone. On New Year's Eve, my grandpa made us throw olive leaves into the fireplace. If the leaf crackled, it meant someone loved us; it was a game of "he loves me, he loves me not." New Year's Day was the day that Saint Basil would come to earth to give the children money. (Saint Basil was our Santa Claus.)

Pappou Savvas loved to laugh, and after his dinner and two glasses of his brother's homemade red wine, he sang traditional Cypriot songs that rhyme, called *chatista*. He also had this talent of making the sound of a wild cat with his lips, and he tricked us often into thinking there was a cat in the house.

My wise grandfather was a good-tempered, honest businessman who was respected by everyone in his village. He often welcomed into his home weary strangers who were passing through the village and gave them a plate of food to eat. To explain how patient *Pappou* Savvas was, I must repeat a story that I was told by my mother. When my grandfather was in his forties, he was sitting in the village coffee shop when a political debate broke out amongst some men. (Political debates are popular amongst older men in Cyprus.) When my grandfather voiced his opinion, an angry neighbor that supported the opposition charged at him like a bull and broke a chair on his head, knocking him unconscious. When he recovered, he was told by all the witnesses to take the violent man to court. The aggressor's wife heard about her husband's behavior from the villagers and ran to my granny's house to apologize on his behalf and beg for my grandfather's forgiveness. My grandfather kept the peace and chose to ignore the nasty incident.

Pappou Savvas's patience stems from his difficult childhood. When he was seven years old, his mother died suddenly of an unknown illness. His father was very poor and could not take care of all his children; one of his younger brothers, Dyonisios, was raised by a childless relative who lived in the city of Nicosia. My grandfather told me that he often walked barefoot to the primary school in the neighboring village because they did not have enough money to buy new shoes. (I wonder if all grandfathers have similar stories.) After school, he worked in the fields to help his father pay off his debt. One of his kind neighbors, a Turkish-Cypriot mother, often gave them a loaf of village bread and some food to eat, and my grandfather learned to speak Turkish. Before the Turkish invasion and devastating war of 1974, Greek and Turkish-Cypriot farmers lived and worked together in harmony, but now Cyprus is divided in two.

In his twenties, *Pappou* Savvas married my grandmother Theodora. In those days, marriages were arranged by the couple's parents. There was no caste system in Cyprus, but inheritance played an important role in choosing a spouse for one's children. My grandparents' marriage was unique because they fell in love. They were fortunate that their families were fond of each other and approved the marriage. My grandmother had a cousin called Athena, whose parents refused to allow her to marry the man she loved because he had no inheritance; she was so devastated that she tried to kill herself. While she was hanging off a tree about to take her final breath, a passerby saved her life by cutting the rope around her neck, and after that day, Athena dedicated her life to God and became a nun.

It was the goal in Cyprus at that time for every family to own one or more pieces of land. They used the land to grow their own food, and they passed it on to their children once they were married. To sell the land that one inherits is still considered disrespectful to many parents. Most Cypriots would rather struggle their whole lives to pay off their debt than sell their precious land. My maternal grandfather started his farming career with empty pockets, but in his lifetime he managed to buy many pieces of land. He farmed every piece of land that he owned with the help of my grandmother and his loyal blue tractor, which was the only vehicle that he ever drove. He paid off all his debt long before he retired. Being the fair person that he was, he left each of his five children an equal amount of land. I can only dream of accomplishing what he did in his lifetime. My maternal grandfather believed in education and sent all his children to high school.

My grandparents built a small house that had only the basic necessities. *Pappou* Savvas continued to use his primitive outside toilet (or hole), even after his eldest son built him a decent bathroom inside his house. To him, the idea of excreting bodily waste inside the house where you slept was ridiculous. My grandfather had no desire to travel or own any luxuries, yet he was the happiest man I have ever known. Our generation always wants more than what we need, and we are never satisfied with what we have. Perhaps it is because we have not felt the hunger pangs of poverty or because we have not lived through a horrifying war, and our biggest concern is the economic crisis? If we all lived simpler lives and learned how to find happiness in nature and our loved ones, there would probably be a lot less stress in the world.

At that time, besides tending to the olive and citrus trees, my father also grew vegetables, grapes, figs, plums, apricots, apples, walnuts, almonds, and he kept beehives and made his own honey. Even though he created great produce, the profit was very low, and he barely made ends meet. In those days, there were few work opportunities in Cyprus. The tourism industry was still in its infancy. The war had taken place in 1974 and the island was struggling to heal its open wounds. Sadly, many Cypriots lost their homes and their loved ones during the war. Thousands of young Greek-Cypriots left their parents and the soil of their birth and went far away to countries like Australia, South Africa, America, and England, either as refugees in search of a better life or in search of the promised "gold." It has been thirty-seven years since the war and the politicians are still struggling to find a solution to the Cyprus problem.

In 1984, my father decided to follow his older brothers and emigrate to South Africa. He was not content with a farmer's salary, and my mother wanted her three children to have a better education than the village could provide. My father's nine older cousins had moved to South Africa in the sixties. They left Cyprus with the clothes on their backs and a few pounds in their pockets, but with hard work, they all managed to do well. My father's older brothers were young teenagers when they left Cyprus. In South Africa they worked long hours for their older cousins, who, in return, provided food, money, and lodging.

Eventually they saved up enough money to start businesses of their own. My generous *Theo* Savvas bought us all tickets to travel to Johannesburg, and he promised to help my father settle and give him work at his supermarket. The family tie is very strong in the Cypriot community, and siblings usually help each other wherever they can. (Occasionally we step on each other's toes, but the war and emigration have taught Cypriots to forgive quickly.)

As our move to South Africa came closer, the day arrived when my father turned our ill-fated pig into tasty *loukanika* [Cypriot pork sausages cured in red wine], *lountza* [pork fillet soaked in red wine, covered with coriander seeds, pressed, and smoked], *sheftalies* [small patties of pork mincemeat, mixed with finely chopped onion, parsley, salt, and pepper, wrapped in pork intestinal skin], and *zalatina* [pig's head, feet, and pork meat boiled, cut into pieces, and preserved with vinegar, lemon juice, spices, and gelatin]. Our chickens and rabbits were given away, and our small house in the village was locked up. My benevolent *Pappou* Savvas took over the responsibility of taking care of my father's trees.

I was six years old at the time, and for me it was all very sad. I cried as I said good-bye to my house, my playing fields, my loving grannies and aunts, and my friendly neighbors that had fed me sweet Cypriot treats ever since I could walk. I waved good-bye to the deep-blue Mediterranean Sea as we passed it on our way to the airport. I wasn't sure when I would see the sea again, and I wondered if I would ever learn how to swim. (I had only been to the sea once before, with overseas relatives who were in Cyprus on holiday, since my parents couldn't swim and never took us to the sea.)

My mother says I sang my favorite chorus in the car: "*Thalassa thalassa, ti mou xeis kanei? Yia sena exasa, kathe limani,*" which means: "My dear sea, what have you done to me? For you, I have missed every harbor."

Chapter 3:

My Primary Years in Big South Africa

I remember landing at the airport in Johannesburg, South Africa. My ears were hurting from the plane ride and probably from the olive-oil-soaked cotton wool my mother had shoved inside them. (If you grew up in a Greek home, you know that olive oil is the cure for everything!) My mother says I cried and stomped my feet like a brat for about an hour. It is a wonder that she sat calmly for nine hours in a plane for the very first time with three young, restless children. My sister Dora was four and a half, and my baby sister, Angela, was two years old. We were bewildered because it was the first time that our innocent eyes saw an African man. (The only people we had met up until then were our white-skinned Cypriot relatives.)

My father smoked cigarette after cigarette while we sat on our luggage and waited for our uncle to fetch us from the airport. (Back then, smoking was, unfortunately, allowed in airports and planes.) My father smoked more when he was anxious or stressed. It must have been a nerve-racking decision for him to move his family to a foreign country with nothing but a suitcase in his hands.

My big-hearted, balding *Theo* Savvas, with his thick black moustache, picked us up in his new Cadillac and took us to his home. He was a bachelor at the time, and he had done very well for himself financially. His house was the biggest that we had ever seen. We met up with the rest of my father's brothers and his sister, who greeted us with delicious homecooked meals. *Theo* Savvas helped my father find a small three-bedroom house and gave him work at his supermarket in a pretty suburb called Alberton. He also gave my father an old, rusty-red Mercedes to drive. He was our savior.

To our delight, our new house, which was built in the Dutch style, had a garden and a small pool. We would learn to swim after all! My mother took out her *kapnistiri* [traditional silver hand smoker], burnt some dried-up olive leaves, and walked around our new house praising God while smoking all the rooms to keep away evil. My mother then approached us, and we each got a turn to fan the smoke toward us three times and make the sign of the cross with our fingers. A few days later, the priest from the Greek Orthodox church of Alberton visited our house to give his blessing. He dipped a few stems of basil leaves in some holy water and sprinkled the water into all the rooms of our new house while he said a prayer. I blinked as some water flew into my eyes.

I was placed in a nursery school across the road from our house, and my mother walked me there every day. I remember feeling very sad as I had no friends and I did not speak any English. To make matters worse, there were twin girls who teased me in Afrikaans (an even more alien language to me). Afrikaans is a language inherited from the first Dutch settlers in South Africa. During our lunch breaks, I hung like a sad puppet on to the school's wall and stared at my new house across the empty field, wishing I were home, where we spoke Greek. Somehow, as children do, I learned to speak English in six months, and it was time for me to start "big" school. My loneliness and struggle to make friends, continued throughout my first few years of primary school. I remember winning my first school prize in grade one for progress. It was a beautiful fairy-tale book, which I cherished and have kept to this day. My mom was so proud. My bilingual buds had started to sprout.

I remember how much I hated athletics day. I was seven years old, had grown up like a wild mountain goat in a village, and yet could not run to save my life. I will never forget the first race the teachers made me run. As soon as the starter gun went off, I tripped, fell on my face, and peed on my gray school dress from shock. The teachers made me get up and keep running. I came in hopelessly last and very ashamed. Thanks to that incident, I still have a phobia of running—that's my excuse for not running, and I'm sticking to it.

My favorite hour at school was story time. I loved listening to the voice of my plump, red-faced, second grade teacher as she read us the story of Charlotte's Web. It reminded me of the magical time I spent with our farm animals in the village. Eventually I learned to read for myself, and that was my escape from reality. In grade three, there was a small bookshelf in my classroom, and the teacher told us that we could read any book we wanted. I sat there during all my breaks, and I eventually read them all. I traveled in the storybooks like one flies around in dreams. I loved reading Roald Dahl's children's books. I read Charlie and the Chocolate Factory, The BFG (Big Friendly Giant), The Witches, James and the Giant Peach, and many more. My English improved, and I won another school prize at the end of the year. By age ten, I would translate all my school letters for my stay-at-home mom.

My mother's English vocabulary was limited, but she remembered a few words from her high school years. Her English improved from speaking to Mary, our Scottish next-door neighbor; my sisters and I spent many hours with Mary's daughters, Michelle and Angela. I also acquired the baffling task of translating letters and bank statements for my father. My father's English was worse than my mother's, and he often mixed up the words I and you—I think that we were the only ones who could understand him. My sisters and I eventually learned to speak Afrikaans, as it was our second compulsory language at school.

One day my younger sister, Dora, came home from nursery school with a big oil stain on her white T-shirt pocket. When my mother asked why her shirt was dirty, she pulled out a half-eaten fish finger from her pocket and said, "Ma, I want you to cook us this thing." My mother had never seen a processed fish finger before. My sister wanted to show her because she loved eating them at nursery school. My mother laughed. The fish that we ate back in Cyprus were whole—complete with their heads and bones in the center. When we were young, we did not realize how lucky we were to have a mother who made us healthy, unprocessed food every single day.

Our father was the early bird in the house, and he was the one who made our breakfast. He made us toast with soft-boiled eggs, sausages, or toasted cheese and ham sandwiches. Our father often dipped our toast in a mixture of olive oil, lemon, oregano, and salt. We begged him to buy us the porridge and cornflakes that we saw advertised on the television. (The first time my family tasted cornflakes was in South Africa.) Our father gave us money to buy hamburgers from the school tuck shop, but we thought that our friends' peanut butter or marmite sandwiches tasted better. As kids, we always craved the food we did not have at home.

While I was in primary school, *Theo* Savvas took us on our first family holiday to show us the wonders of the big country that had become our new home. We swallowed our anti-malaria tablets, piled into my uncle's minivan, and went on a road trip to the Kruger National Park. Naturally, my Cypriot parents packed a gas burner, Greek coffee, homemade rusks, *halloumi* cheese which some relative had brought from Cyprus, boiled eggs, and a Tupperware container filled with olives to snack on during the long drive to the game reserve. During our safari we saw many wild animals, including the famous big five—the cheetah, buffalo, lion, elephant, and rhinoceros. Our uncle ignited our African education when he told us that the cheetah is the fastest land animal. My favorite animals were the tall, odd-looking giraffes. On our way out, an enormous angry elephant stopped in the middle of the road and flapped its ears until we backed off. It was great fun sleeping in a thatch-roofed hut and waking up to the laughter of monkeys that were stealing garbage outside our door.

Our uncle then drove us six hours away to show us the coast of Durban. We watched the men fish in the rough Indian Ocean while we built sand castles and collected seashells. On the way back home, we passed a few African huts and bought hand-sculpted wooden elephants from the locals. *Theo* Savvas made one more stop to cut a few sticks of sugarcane from a field. We chewed on the sugarcane for hours, trying to suck out as much sweetness as we could.

A few years later my mother's youngest sister, Maria, and her brother Aki joined us in South Africa, and we spent most weekends together. *Thea* Maria eventually married Uncle Costa, and we were delighted when we were made flower girls. *Thea* Maria and Uncle Costa lived with us for a few months until they could support themselves. In those days, my uncle Costa wore thick glasses and had a beard and dark, curly hair. When he was young, he used sticky tape to glue his thick, broken glasses together because his Cypriot parents did not have enough money to buy him new ones. When he was older, he worked long hours doing all sorts of jobs and saved up as much money as he could. He used his savings to buy a tiny, run-down butchery in his hometown of Boksburg, and, being the driven man that he is, he turned it into a great success.

Uncle Costa was an intelligent man who loved to read, and he always knew the answers to all our questions. He was our human 'Wikipedia'. He was also our savior on the weekends because he took us on many fun outings; our father was always busy working at that time. Our new uncle took us to the Gold Reef City theme park, where we went down into a mine and learned how gold is mined in South Africa and where we watched traditional Zulu dancing. Every year he took us to the Rand Show, which was a big exhibition that sold everything for the home and had many exhilarating rides that we loved. He took us to see the colorful musical fountains and to Bruma Lake, a big flea market with many food stalls that was situated around a lake. He introduced us to delicious South African food like *boerewors* [sausages made with beef and pork, seasoned with spices like coriander, along with wine and vinegar], *mielie-pap* [a starchy mash made with maize flour], *biltong* [like American jerky, only better; it is made with various game meats and spices] and *koeksisters* [sweet, syrupy plaited doughnuts]. My uncle also arranged many fun picnics or *braais* [barbecues] in massive green parks like Heidelberg Kloof.

Since we lived in a foreign country, my parents did not want us to forget our Greek roots. While my female classmates attended ballet lessons after school, my sisters and I attended Greek school four days a week. At that time, we resented the extra work, but today we are grateful because we can speak the language fluently and read and write basic Greek. We also learned about our traditions, religion, history, and culture. A patriotic friend of ours wore a badge of a Greek flag on his school blazer, and he would annoy his South African friends by bragging about how cool it was to be Greek. In South Africa we were probably more Greek than the Greeks in Greece, and we were always having festivals to celebrate our "Greekness." Our Greek friends teased us often about our Cypriot dialect, telling us we spoke funny. A lot of Cypriot words are different from the Greek because we still use a few ancient Greek words, and a few of our words have been inherited from all the nations that occupied Cyprus in the past. We can understand the Greek language perfectly, but the Greeks do not always understand us. My youngest sister, Angela, adapted more to her South African friends and hated everything Greek, and so she bunked Greek school often.

Growing up, we had many pets, but for various reasons they did not

live very long. I remember our excitement when our father bought home a shoe box containing three yellow, fluffy chicks that one of his customers had given him as a gift. We took care of the baby chickens as if they were precious stones. It was not long before the greedy chicks grew into big, fat chickens and my father was forced to build a small chicken pen in our garden. I arrived home one afternoon, only to find three headless, bloody hens running around our garden. My father was tired of their squawking and my mother decided it was time to make *trahana* [chicken soup]. My parents were not great pet lovers —the only pets they had growing up were farm animals that they eventually ate. Even though I cried over the fate of the hens, I still ate my mother's delicious chicken soup.

When I was eleven years old, I met Jennifer, a blond, Scottish girl with sky-blue eyes. Friendly and kind to me, Jennifer became my first best friend. My sisters and I spent many afternoons at her house after school. At that time, Jennifer was the only non-Greek friend we were allowed to visit, besides our next-door neighbor. Jennifer's intelligent mother, Liz, taught us geography and made us play fun, mind-stimulating games. Compared to our unathletic family, Jennifer and her three sisters were very courageous. At ten years old, her sister Cheryl was the youngest pilot in South Africa, and she could fly a plane with an instructor. Jennifer could paraglide off a hill at the age of eleven, and she knew how to steer a canoe in a fastflowing river. Jennifer taught me how to ride a bicycle. My sisters and I never owned a bicycle because our overprotective father was afraid we would fall off and get killed, or get kidnapped. My friend's mother took us to the movies and to the bowling alley for the very first time, as those recreational acts were alien to my parents. Sadly for me, Jennifer and her family moved back to Scotland just before we started high school, but we became the greatest pen pals. Since e-mail was nonexistent at that time, we wrote letters to each other on decorated or scented pieces of paper and sent them by post. (My nephews will think I am ancient after reading that.)

When I turned twelve, I finally became a woman. Having my first period was a shocking, painful experience. I ran inside to tell my mother and was smacked on the cheek. She said, "That is the Cyprus tradition—for you not to be scared." My mother then proceeded to show me how to use a sanitary pad, which was the size of a nappy. I had heard some girls at school talking about tampons, and I asked my mother about them. She shouted, "No, you crazy! These things evil. They take away virginity, and no Greek man want to marry you!" My mom scared the living daylights out of me, and I never dared try them. My mother made me drink many cups of homegrown mint tea, which did little to soothe my terrible menstrual cramps.

Another downfall to being a young Cypriot girl was that I had the hairiest legs of all the girls in my class, because my mother did not want us to shave our legs at a young age. I was so hairy that while I was singing away in the shower one day, a huge praying mantis attached itself to my leg hairs and started heading north. As hard as I kicked, I could not shake the insect off, and I had to pull it off with my fingers. After that awful day, I snuck behind my mother's back, stole my father's razor, and shaved for the very first time. I cut myself badly, but at least my legs no longer resembled a baboon's. Since then, I have developed an obsession for finding the best hair removal treatment available—the curse of all dark-haired women. My first bikini wax was the defining moment in my life when I understood the meaning of the saying "pain for beauty."

During my school years, I suffered regularly with tonsillitis—that painful throat infection that makes it impossible to taste and swallow food. Those were the few days in my life when I couldn't eat my mother's food. My protective father rushed me to the doctor on a monthly basis, and the doctor got rid of us by prescribing his usual antibiotic. Today I am resistant to five different antibiotics. To ease my sore throat, my father made me drink hot mint tea with lemon juice and honey, and he made me gargle with some olive oil. My father's cure for everything else was Vick's Vapo Rub, which was sold in their supermarket in South Africa. It is a type of petroleum jelly mixed with strong-smelling eucalyptus oil. When we had a cough, blocked nose, headache, or fever, he made us rub the ointment on our chest, back, and under our nose. We even used it to cure the itch from a mosquito bite.

Fortunately for us, our father did not believe in corporal punishment, even though he was part of the special-forces during his compulsory army years in Cyprus. He never lifted his hand to smack any of us. All he had to do was raise his voice a notch or two, and our tears would flow like a running tap. Our mother was not as sympathetic as our father when we misbehaved, and she chased after us with her slipper or rolling pin. We escaped by jumping into our swimming pool because we knew our mother couldn't swim—we did that until she got smart and started using the pool brush.

Our rusty, red Mercedes was abandoned only when it broke down. Our father then bought a used snotgreen Chevrolet, which was the ugliest car we had ever seen. He drove us to school in his prized Chevrolet every morning. Around every corner, the left back door of his old car would swing open, and we had to hold tight to keep from falling out. We would duck down when we reached our school and sneak out; to annoy us, our father dropped us off right in front by the school gate where all the popular kids stood. My father was always in a hurry to rush off to work, and on more than one occasion he drove over my sister's foot in his haste. (Thanks to strong, hard school shoes, my sister still has both her feet.)

Our mother finally passed her driving test (after my father bribed the instructor), and she took over driving us to school. She drove like a snail because she was nervous, and, in her daze, she often drove off before we had a chance to grab all our school bags from the trunk. We would run after our car, yelling for our mother to stop, while the kids at the school gate had a good laugh.

During those years, we spent very little time with our father. He became a workaholic, partly out of necessity and partly because it is in an immigrant's nature. He worked Monday to Saturday, 7:00 a.m. until 9:00 p.m., and until noon on Sundays and public holidays. Eventually my father earned his own shares in the supermarket and became a partner with his brothers. Unfortunately, things did not go as planned because the big supermarket was engulfed by a mountain of debt. My father sold our house in Cyprus for peanuts (as my mother would say), and he used the money to help with the supermarket's debt. (To this day, my mother has not forgiven him for selling their home in Cyprus.) Due to necessity, the supermarket was eventually sold, and after a short venture in the casino business my father bought his own little grocery store.

Every Sunday afternoon, our father made up for lost family time by making us his mouthwatering *souvla*. This is a Cypriot barbecue with big pieces of lamb, pork, or chicken seasoned with salt, wild oregano, and fresh lemon juice. The meat pieces are placed on a skewer that is turned slowly over hot charcoal until the fat is nice and crispy. You can take the Cypriot out of Cyprus, but you can never take the *souvla* out of the Cypriot! *Souvla* tastes the best when it is eaten straight off the fire while it is still hot, with a squeeze of fresh lemon. Did you know that when you add lemon to meat, the vitamin C the lemon contains brings out the iron in the meat and helps the body to absorb it better?

On Sundays, our father also cut the grass and tended to our perfectly groomed garden. A friend of ours used to call him Superman because he would arrive home from work and, in a flash, he was out of his work clothes, into his garden shorts, and outside pushing his lawn mower. My father will always have green fingers—it is in his blood. He plants and prunes every type of plant that one can imagine. In our little garden in South Africa, he grew two kinds of beans, two kinds of melons, lettuce, cabbage, *rokka* [rocket plants], *kouloumbres* [kohlrabi], various green herbs, watercress, *glysteridha* [purslane], pumpkin, marrows, zucchini, peppers, onions, cucumbers, and tomatoes. We also had fig, plum, apricot, lemon, and olive trees, and an impressive entwined grapevine shading our courtyard. We had the neatest and most productive garden in the neighborhood. You could always distinguish a Greek home from a South African one by the row of olive trees in the front yard.

My father always gave more affection to his trees than he did to our mother. Whenever our mother nagged in his ears, he made a quick escape to his garden. I have never seen my conservative parents hug, kiss, or even hold hands. (I can only assume that these acts take place behind closed doors.) The words "I love you" were not spoken in our house, but we did not need the words because we felt loved. Because my father felt guilty that he worked many hours and spent so little time with us, he spoiled us with chocolates, crisps, soft drinks, and plenty of sweets from his grocery store. As a result, we spent many long hours at the dentist's office.

Although my father was very generous with sweets, he was very strict about how much toilet paper we used. "Two blocks a time. Fold and wipe, and fold and wipe—make little *economia*!" he would shout. He went mad if we left lights on in empty rooms, and we were not allowed to leave the water running while we brushed our teeth. He grew up in poverty and hated to see us waste anything. Ironically, though, like his brothers and many of the Cypriots in South Africa, he did not mind spending his hard-earned money in the addictive casinos. My father has a great mistrust of priests, and he is not a religious man at all, so on the Sundays when he said, "Hokay, come everybody. We go to church," we knew he was not talking about the house of God.

Our father would drive us to his favorite casino, which was two hours away and called Sun City. It was the biggest casino resort in South Africa and was built by Sol Kerzner. It had everything necessary to entertain young and old. While my father was glued to the roulette table for hours, trying to win the jackpot, we wandered off with our mother, our *Thea* Maria, and Uncle Costa. We enjoyed the kids' games, the pools, the man-made beach, the movies, the restaurants, and the wild birds and monkeys in the magnificent gardens. When my father won in the casino, it was a happy day for all because he gave us pocket money. When he lost, he was miserable and swore to himself in Greek and incorrect English all the way back home.

Our mother was the one that took us to real church. Every year during Holy Week of the Greek Orthodox Easter, our mother made us give up all animal products. We were not allowed to eat any type of meat, eggs, or dairy product. The ideal fasts are supposed to start fifty days before Easter and forty days before Christmas. In order to take Holy Communion in the Greek Orthodox Church, one has to have fasted for at least three days. Some days during the fasting week, I would cheat and eat chocolate at school, but I always felt as though a holy lightning bolt was going to strike my head. There was a very brief moment when I thought about becoming a nun, and I started reading the Bible. I found fasting for forty days to be too difficult, and Mother

Teresa quickly left my mind.

The point of fasting is to purify the body as well as the soul by sacrificing food for God and being a good Christian. Every year on Holy Friday, which represents Jesus's Crucifixion, a wooden altar is decorated with many colorful flowers and carried around the Greek Orthodox Church while we follow the procession. On Holy Saturday we take special candles to the church and receive the Holy Light that comes from the priest's candle after his prayers to God. The Holy Light is passed around the church to all the faithful. We take the Holy Light home and use it to burn a cross on the wall above the entrance of our house to keep away evil. When we were young, we could not wait for the Saturday night church service, which carries on until after midnight, to be over. One minute past twelve, it is Easter Sunday, and we go home to break our fast with a delicious chicken and rice soup, made with a lemon and egg froth, called *avgolemoni*. *Thea* Anna and *Thea* Eleni, my mother's best friends from Greece, make a similar soup but with lamb tripe, heart, liver, lettuce and a few green herbs like dill, spring onions, and parsley. The Greeks call their Easter soup *mayeritsa*. After breaking our fast, we say, "*Christos Anesti*," which means, "Christ has risen." We knock hard-boiled eggs that are painted red to see whose egg is the strongest.

There are several stories about why we paint our eggs red during Easter. As a child, I was told that after Jesus's Crucifixion and Resurrection, a faithful Christian lady walked through the streets shouting, "Christ has risen!" A passing Roman soldier overheard her and told her that if that was true, the basket of eggs that she was holding should turn red, and they miraculously did. Others say that the red color represents the blood that was shed by Christ during the Crucifixion. Today we use all sorts of colors to paint our eggs.

Every Easter Sunday, Christmas, and New Year's Day, we would get together with our huge extended family and have a heavenly feast. We would enjoy either a baby pig, stuffed with garlic, sprinkled with herbs, and brushed repeatedly with lemon juice and olive oil, slow cooked on a spit, or my father's famous lamb *souvla*. During Easter, we also ate my mother's *tsoureki*, which is a kind of sweet bread similar to Italian panettone, and *flaounes*, which are triangular Cypriot Easter rolls that are filled with a mixture of eggs, different cheeses, spices, and raisins and sprinkled with sesame seeds. On New Year's Day, we looked forward to my father cutting our mother's *vasilopitta*. This is a dry, orange-scented tea cake that has a coin hidden inside it; whoever finds the coin in his or her slice has good luck for the rest of the year.

There was always enough food at our family gatherings to feed an army. My parents and relatives took turns hosting the holiday lunches. The chain-smoking men prepared the meat and played poker while the women sat separately to gossip and exchange recipes. Strangely, my relatives seem to avoid mixing genders at family gatherings.

After lunch, my entertaining *Thea* Maria read our fortunes by looking into our small Greek coffee cups. (You stop drinking Greek coffee once you get to the sandy bit, and then you turn your cup over in its saucer to dry.) She would say, "You have an admirer and his name starts with the letter M. Look, do you see the letter in your cup?" To another she would say, "Your cup looks clear today—that means no worries in your house." It was the only reason I forced myself to drink strong Greek coffee! After coffee, it was time for cake. Each of my aunts would bring a homemade dessert, and I think there was a secret competition to see who made the best one. The winner was made obvious when the first dish was emptied out.

Thea Maria made the best carrot cake and pavlova [a meringue covered with fresh cream, fresh strawberries, kiwi fruit, and banana]. On Saturdays my aunt made me rub olive oil in her thick, brown hair because she believed it would make her hair stronger. (I must confess that today, *Thea* Maria has the most hair of all of us.) My sisters and I loved to sleep over at her house and babysit our young cousins: Dimitri, who we called Mimi, Savvaki, and Yiannaki. Dimitri's first word was Enena—his attempt at my name. By age twelve, I was an expert at changing nappies and making milk formula. My cousin Savvaki was born with blond hair and blue eyes—our family's missing link to the ancient Greeks that once lived in Cyprus. My baby cousin Yiannaki would get confused and call me "Ma" when he started to talk.

My beautiful, red-haired *Thea* Artemis (*Theo* Savvas's wife) dressed glamorously in high heels and tailored skirts; she had voluptuous curves and looked just like Sophia Loren. She taught us how to use lip and eye- liner for the first time and made homemade face creams and masks out of Greek yogurt, honey, and various fruits. She also brewed healthy herbal teas and made the best *lokoumades* [Cypriot honey balls], which were little balls of dough that were fried until golden and dipped in fragrant, sweet syrup or honey.

While we waited for our *lokoumades*, my sisters and I explored their beautiful, mysterious mansion. It had two kitchens, two lounge areas, two dining rooms, a bar area, a secret hunting closet, and about six bedrooms. It had a swimming pool adorned with statues of the Greek gods, a tennis court, a sauna, and an outside entertainment area. It also had a huge garage with six cars parked inside and a silver disco ball on the roof. Our five-year-old cousin, Omeros, had his own miniature Ferrari, which he drove around the yard.

Once a week we would visit our beloved *Theo* Savvas at his restaurant, the Promise Grill. My father never even considered eating out at any other restaurant, but we didn't mind because the food was fantastic. We ate the most delicious steaks, prawns, oysters, creamed spinach, garlic snails, Greek salad, and ice cream with hot chocolate sauce. Out of necessity my uncle eventually sold his restaurant and his mansion and moved with his family to Cape Town.

My loving godfather, Jimmy, is another of my father's brothers. He is overweight because of his wife's (my godmother Alexandra's) delicious cooking. I remember hearing him snore very loudly whenever I slept over at their house. My stylish godmother loved fashion and shopping for designer dresses. There is a holy corner in their house where she prays and lights an oil lantern every day for the icon of the Virgin Mary. My godmother made the best *kateyfi*, which is a dessert of stringy, thin spaghetti dough with almonds in the center that is covered in sweet syrup and baked until crispy. When we were kids, I played "school school" with my god-sister (my godmother's daughter), Julie, who had a blackboard and pretended to be my teacher. She also had a telescope, and we took it out at night and searched for aliens on the bright moon. Julie's younger brother, Miriko, was my naughtiest cousin, and I remember him getting into trouble for bunking school and shooting the neighborhood cats with his pellet gun. We always joked that he would join the mafia when he was older, but today he loves animals and nature and has become a real 'Crocodile Dundee'.

Thea Christalla (my dad's sister) made the tastiest baby potatoes. They were fried in olive oil and tossed with coriander seeds, salt, and fresh lemon juice. She also made various perfect cakes. She lived across the road from us and had the tidiest and cleanest house. We danced to Kylie Minogue's "The Locomotion" with our cousins Christina and Haritini, and we entertained their younger brother Dino.

My gentle, soft-spoken *Thea* Helen was married to my father's youngest brother, Uncle Theo, and she made the best cheesecake and chocolate mousse. Sadly, *Thea* Helen died from ovarian cancer when she was only forty years old. God rest her soul. My uncle Theo had to take care of his young boys, Savvas, age ten, and Paul, age nine, on his own after that. My parents helped out whenever they could. Uncle Theo learned how to cook, and he now makes his own strawberry jam and the best chocolate cake I have ever tasted—no small feat for a Cypriot man. My uncle did the best he could raising my young cousins. He must have loved my aunt very much, because he has not remarried. We also loved to visit my laid-back *Theo* Aki, my mother's brother, at his supermarket in Krugersdorp, which was an hour away from our house. He spoiled us with sweets and chocolates and allowed us free access to his store's video games. My modern *Thea* Despina (Uncle Aki's wife) was a graceful ballet and tap-dancing teacher with long, raven-black hair. She makes the best *mousaka*, which is a Greek dish that is made with eggplant, zucchini, potatoes, and minced meat that is covered with béchamel sauce and baked in the oven. My aunt bought her children, Irene and Aristos, many toys. Irene's room looked like Toyland, and when we were there, we thought we were in heaven.

Even though most of my uncles never attended high school or college, they were all self-made, successful businessmen, and for many years they worked very hard to provide their families a good quality of life.

At this point I would like to say a few words about my female relatives. Besides being great cooks and excellent housekeepers, they have also been loyal wives to their husbands, and they have been married for twenty-five years or more. I believe that the longevity of their marriages is attributed to the fact that most Cypriot women from my mother's generation are very tolerant. They know how to forgive, they believe that marriage is for life even when it feels like a curse, and they always put their children's needs first. Their husbands and children are very lucky to have them. I have heard a saying that holds true for most Cypriot couples: the man is the head of the house, but the woman is the neck that turns the head whichever way she wants.

When I was about twelve years old, our father sent us on our first holiday back to Cyprus (naturally, he stayed behind to work). As we stepped off the aircraft at Larnaca Airport, we were hit by a blast of heat and humidity. I inhaled deeply, and the air awoke a sense of nostalgia in my soul which brought back fond childhood memories. (Anyone who lives abroad and returns to his or her birthplace will understand that emotion.) After a three-hour drive, we entered the familiar territory of our mother's village of Steni.

It was great to reunite with our grandparents after many years of being apart. Our Cypriot relatives were constantly trying to feed us. When we refused the food they offered, their faces would scrunch up in disappointment, so most of the time we ate rather than hurt their feelings. They told us we were too skinny and that we weren't eating enough in South Africa. *Yiayia* Theodora was happiest when she cooked our favorite Cypriot dishes, and she praised us daily with her blessings. We spent a few days with my mom's sister, *Thea* Vathoulla, who lives next door to our granny. She kept a chicken pen and made the tastiest roast chicken; it was covered with slices of potatoes, ripe tomatoes, and onions, and sprinkled with spices like cinnamon, pepper, and salt. We spent many hours entertaining her young children, Dimitri and Maria.

I reunited with my childhood friend Noni, who lived up the road from my granny's house. She was my best friend in Cyprus, and for years she was the pen pal with whom I practiced my Greek writing and shared my secret crushes. I knew all the old ladies in Steni village, and as I walked past their houses to visit my friend, one by one they called out, *"Kopiase"* ["Come in to eat"] and invited me in to taste their homemade Cypriot sweets. After eating my fourth sweet bergamot peel, I had to politely turn them down. They asked me if I knew their relatives in South Africa and proceeded to list all their names—they assumed that all Cypriots overseas knew each other. I noticed that they all had African animal souvenirs on their shelves and the same copper clock, painted with the big five, hanging on their walls. Occasionally Noni picked me up with her sister's scooter and we drove through the village, overtaking old ladies on their donkeys.

When my sisters and I wanted to go to the sea, which was a fifteen-minute drive away, we would simply hitchhike. We could never do that in South Africa, but in Cyprus it was safe, as we knew everyone in the village. The drivers that stopped were more than happy to drop us off, and they were usually related to my parents somehow or other. They recognized me straight away and told me I looked just like my mother or other times just like my father.

Occasionally we walked with our granny to the house of her sister, our great-aunt Maria. She welcomed us with open arms and took out her flat, burnt-black frying pan to make us her specialty—*katimeria*. This is flat, square-shaped dough that is pan fried in a little olive oil until golden brown and then sprinkled with honey or sugar. My great aunt's garden was filled with beautiful orchids and roses that her husband, unshaven *Theo* Loizo, sold to the tourists in the town. Whenever *Theo* Loizo saw us, he gave us long-stemmed red roses as a gift. My great aunt Maria passed away recently, but before she died she gave me some pot plants filled with orchid bulbs, and when they are in bloom, they remind me of her kind and generous spirit.

My mother's oldest brother, *Theo* Fito, is a respected policeman; he took us sightseeing on his days off. One day, he took us to Saint Neofitos Monastery in Paphos. We climbed many steps to see a secret cave that was dug out of a rocky mountain by a devoted hermit. This was where he lived, prayed, and painted religious icons on the walls. Many faithful people would visit the hermit and ask for his prayers for their sick loved ones; after his death, he became a saint because a few of the sick were healed.

Another time *Theo* Fito drove us to the mountains of Panayia, where we hiked on a secluded nature trail in a pine forest. After forty-five minutes we reached a rock that had a large indentation in the center. Crystal-clear water dripped continuously inside this rock, and it formed a shaded pool. We drank the water to quench our thirst, and it was cool, sweet, and refreshing. The story behind this rock was that a saint was passing through the forest carrying a large icon of the Virgin Mary. When the saint grew weary and thirsty, the Virgin Mary told him to punch a hole in the rock. A hole miraculously opened and filled with water for the saint to drink. The rock has been dripping water ever since.

During our last weekend, Uncle Fito took us to our favorite beach in Latchi for a swim. We were with his young children, Savva, Ioanna, and Fitoulla. As we started swimming in the sea, we noticed a whole family of nudists standing a few meters away next to a big rock. The grandparents, parents, and children were all stark naked. It was the first time my sisters and I had seen a naked man in the flesh, and we didn't know whether to laugh or cry. My uncle casually walked out of the sea, put his police hat on, and went to politely tell the tourists to put their swimming costumes back on.

On the long flight back to South Africa, my sisters and I, whether we liked it or not, carried a ten-kilo kitbag each. Our kitbags were filled with a big bottle of homemade olive oil, a few small bottles of green olives, bunches of wild oregano, a few packets of *halloumi* cheese, bottles of pickled Cyprus capers, bottles of sweet *karithaki*, a few packets of *loukanika, lountza*, and *tsamarella* (similar to jerky but made with mature goat's meat, wild oregano, and a lot of salt), a few bottles of my granny's *mosfilo* jam, and a loaf of village bread. Ah, the good old days before September 11, when you could travel with a year's supply of food for all your relatives in your hand luggage! The country in which one is born draws the soul back like a magnet and never lets the taste buds forget it. My sisters and I also wore an evil eye around our neck—you know, to keep away those evil spirits and keep the plane from falling down. We had many blessings and regards to give our father from all three of our loving grannies.

Unfortunately, at that time the crime in South Africa was escalating. One night my father had a nightmare that he had four guns held to his head by four robbers. He woke up in a sweat. When he went to work that morning, he called his friends from the local police station and asked them to keep an eye on the shop. The policemen ate the pizza and drank the beer that my dad had offered them, and as they saw no sign of trouble, they left. Half an hour later, four men with black hoods over their heads walked into the shop with AK-47 rifles and pointed them at my father's head. He immediately opened the store's safe, and the robbers filled their bags with all the money. They took jewels and watches from the shocked customers. As they turned to leave, one of the store customers bent down to grab a gun that was hidden in his sock. He was shot in the face; the bullet went into his cheek and out of his ear—miraculously, he survived.

Most of the neighbors in our quiet suburb had been robbed, and it was dangerous to walk our dog around the block. The low, wavy brick walls of our front yard were replaced with high, dangerously spiky metal gates. After a burglar jumped into our backyard from a neighbor's wall, my father placed barbed wire on the top of all the surrounding walls of our house. We had burglar bars on all our windows, and a security guard drove around every hour to check on our house. We became prisoners in our own home. My father was afraid for us, and we were afraid for him. Our father was robbed a total of four times, and on one occasion he was even shot at. He is lucky to be alive. I believe it was my granny's prayers that kept us safe all those years.

Because of the racist apartheid regime, South Africa was in a big mess. Such a beautiful country with so much to offer, and yet racism, crime, and poverty were rife. When I was fourteen years old, I wrote this poem for school:

> *South Africa, why do you frown?*
> *Clear up your tears before you drown.*
> *Blood is splattered on your face,*
> *and weeping mothers wear black lace.*
> *You have created one big war,*
> *between two colors, nothing more.*

In 1990, Nelson Mandela was released from prison. It was an exciting but hair-raising time. My paranoid father thought there was going to be a violent war between the African freedom fighters and the extremist Afrikaners; a few weeks before Nelson Mandela's release, he stocked up our pantry with tinned fish and canned beans—as if we would ever starve. Thanks to the peaceful, forgiving, and wise nature of Nelson Mandela, there was no war in our suburb. My father and all our relatives relaxed. Nelson Mandela reminded me of my grandfather Savvas, because he was also humble, patient, and down-to-earth. That year African children joined our public school, and African people finally had the right to vote and own their own homes anywhere in South Africa. The unfair apartheid regime was over. We did not realize it at the time, but we were witnesses to a great historical event.

Chapter 4:

Surviving Adolescence in High School

We attended ordinary public schools, which were a ten-minute drive away from our house. I cherish my high school years because of the laughter I shared with my friends. We had a group of boys in our class who constantly got up to mischief and had us in stitches every day. Their bottoms are probably indented from the hidings they got from our strict Afrikaans deputy principal, who beat them with a hard wooden stick. One day the boys pretended there was a mouse in our mathematics classroom. They had our teacher standing on her chair, screaming with fear, while they ran around the room pretending to catch the invisible mouse. In biology class, my classmate (and second cousin) Chris pretended that his contact lens had fallen to the floor. The boys distracted the lesson for half an hour pretending to look for the contact lens. Chris never wore contact lenses.

I was not interested in romancing boys like most of the girls in my class. All they seemed to care about was how many guys they could scribble on their kissing list, which I thought was really gross. I had no idea what first or second base meant. Even though I enjoyed male attention, I played hard to get with the boys, as if I were a Greek goddess. My protective Uncle Costa put the fear of God in me when he told me that teenage boys were dirty animals and only had sex on their brain. When I was fifteen, I remember my cousin Chris throwing a big party at his parents' house. My classmates and I were sitting on the carpet playing spin the bottle. When the bottle stopped spinning, the girl was supposed to kiss the boy it was pointing to and vice versa. At some stage, it was my turn to spin the bottle. To my relief, Chris's conservative, no-nonsense Cypriot father suddenly walked into the room. Chris panicked, grabbed the empty Coke bottle, threw it behind his back, and poked the girl sitting next to him. With a straight face, he shouted, "Touch, you're on!" He pretended we were playing an innocent game. I laughed until my stomach hurt. It was obviously not my fate to kiss a boy in high school.

Like all teenagers, I had my fair share of complexes. I hated my thousand and one pimples, and I tried every acne cream and potion under the sun. I hated my aquiline Greek nose, and I slept with my finger pushed up against it, hoping that in the morning it would be smaller. I thought a jumbo jet could land on my forehead. My mother tried to make me feel better by telling me I had a large forehead because I was clever, and had a huge brain. My sisters and I had many catfights and teased each other where we knew it hurt. My sisters were nothing like me; they hated studying and reading books, and they preferred to follow the latest fashion and music instead. We acquired roles in our family: I was the smart one, Dora was the pretty one, and Angela was more than happy to be the "baby" of leisure. Relatives (God bless them) can really mess with your sensitive teenage brain by complimenting your sister's beauty and patting you on the back for getting good grades.

Somehow, throughout high school I was in the top twelve students in my class—without any help from my parents or extra lessons. However, I always envied the top three students. My grades could have been better, but I always left my studying for the day before my exams. (I often woke up at three o' clock in the morning on the day of the exam, just to get through all my work.) I must have been one of the few pupils in my class that did not have a computer at home. Trying to explain to my parents how important a computer is remains hopeless. To this day, my father thinks computers are a waste of energy, and my mother tells me I will go blind from staring at my computer screen. My mother drove me to the local library when we had school projects to research; there was no such thing as 'the internet' in our home. I decided that since I hadn't inherited the traits of a supermodel, I had to get good grades in order to find a decent job in the future. My dream was to earn enough money to be able to work fewer hours than my father, and to one day be able to travel the world and taste new, exciting foods.

In high school, I finally found a sport that I was good at—Greek dancing. *Kiria* [Mrs.] Mary, our dancing teacher, was a short, well-groomed woman in her sixties who always wore heels. Her reputation as the best Greek dancing teacher in South Africa was irrefutable. Our dancing lessons were held at the Greek community hall on Saturday mornings. We learned dances from all the Greek islands, including Cyprus, and we danced in big groups at festivals and dancing competitions. It amazed me how our teacher remembered all the steps to so many different dances. My favorite dances were the Zorba and the fast, heart-pounding dances from Crete. My sisters gave up on Greek dancing because *Kiria* Mary would pull them by the arm and lift them off the ground every time they missed a step. She showed no mercy when her students did not concentrate on their steps. Because I had rhythm and was taller than the other girls, I was in her good books. *Kiria* Mary has taught dancing to three generations of South African Greeks and is still teaching to this day.

Our old-fashioned father did not want our mother to work outside our home. Our mother grew tired of being the obedient housewife and tried all sorts of things to keep busy and earn extra money. She knitted, did needlework, embroidered tapestries and lacy tablecloths, painted ceramics, learned how to decoupage, and sold Tupperware. She completed an Italian dressmaking course and sewed gorgeous dresses and suits for our female relatives and for many ladies that she met at our Greek school. Our mother's placid nature made her a magnet for attracting loyal friends.

At that time, our mother started preparing our *brika* [dowry]—another manic Cypriot tradition. She bought each of us a huge box and filled it with an equal number of pots, porcelain plates, kitchen utensils, sheets, and all sorts of useful Tupperware. My mother planned to give us our dowry when we were married. If you visit my married sisters and female cousins, you will find that, to our dismay, our kitchen cupboards are overfilled with exactly the same old-fashioned pots and plates!

Our mother's main mission during our high school years was to make her daughters good housewives, or **kales nikokires** as they say in Greek. She fought with us constantly to clean up the house, just in case guests were to arrive unannounced. We were not as fortunate as most middle-class South Africans that had a live-in maid. When our doorbell rang, my sisters and I ran around like headless chickens, making sure the house was clean and tidy before we opened the door; an amusing sight to see but not very pleasant for the annoyed guests who were waiting outside. Like most houses in our suburb, we had two lounge rooms—one where the family watched TV and one meticulously kept room that my mother reserved for guests.

One afternoon, my sister Dora and I had a huge argument over who was going to wash the dishes. She ran to her room, and I ran after her, trying to convince her that it was her turn. My excuse to get out of dishwashing was always the same—I had to study. She slammed the door in my face, and I caught my middle finger in the door lock by mistake. Dora proceeded to lock the door on my caught finger. When I pulled my finger out, the tip and nail were missing and blood oozed out like a mini fountain. I begged Dora to open the door so that I could find the other half of my finger, but she thought I was bluffing. Only when she heard my mother's hysterical screams did she open the door. On the way to the hospital, I studied the anatomy of my severed finger and thought it was fascinating. My apologetic sister found the missing piece of my finger, with its long, manicured nail, on the floor of her room. The doctor said it could not be sewn back on, but I was very fortunate that my nail grew back, and my shortened finger healed after a few weeks. For a few weeks, I walked around school with a bandaged middle finger, which my friends found very amusing.

Every week, *Yiayia* Theodora in Cyprus used the local phone booth by the village coffee shop to call us and make sure that we were safe. When we called my granny from South Africa, someone from the coffee shop ran to her house to let her know. My maternal grandparents only installed a telephone in their house just before I finished high school. When mobile phones first became popular, I must have been about sixteen. We were spellbound by our father's banana phone, even though it was about the same size as a brick. My selfless *Pappou* Savvas deposited money in my mother's bank account in Cyprus every time he sold the oranges from my father's trees. He never kept any profit for himself, even though he was the one that tended the trees. My mother wept every time she spoke to her parents on the phone; her nostalgia was immense. We were told that one day we would move back to our birthplace. We missed our grandparents and the sparkling Mediterranean Sea.

When I was sixteen and still a romantic soul, I wrote this poem:

Mediterranean Sea
You call me and invade my dreams,
like you engulf the sun and steal her beams.
I stare into your deep blue eyes,
And, hypnotized, believe your lies.
Your foamy arms are pulling me,
and all I hear is your desperate plea.
I yearn to feel your soothing touch,
and taste your salt, which cures so much.
You have accomplished your one wish,
I thirst for you like a stranded fish.

On weekends, I waitressed at my uncle's restaurant, the Promise Grill. My mother's cousin Yianni bought the restaurant from **Theo** Savvas, and it remained in the family. I learned to communicate well with the customers in order to make very good tips. That was my first job. The first night I waitressed, my kind uncle Yianni told me that I could order anything from the menu to eat during my break. I ordered the lobster thermidor and the other waiters looked at me very strangely. I was so naive about the cost of food that my uncle probably regretted his words. I had no idea that the letters S.Q. on the menu implied price on request. When I discovered the price of the lobster, I felt so embarrassed that I wanted to turn into liquid and hide amongst the stains in the carpet beneath my feet. From then on, I stuck to ordering my dinner from the cheaper children's menu—but the sweet taste of the expensive lobster lingered on my taste buds.

In high school we started going to Greek socials and clubs with our older cousins, and Greek friends, who drove cars. On weekends, we begged our mother to let us go out, but every time we asked, she simply said, "No!" So, being Daddy's girls, we turned to our father and managed to twist his rubber arm. We thought we had great talent getting into clubs while underage. I was always the responsible bodyguard of my younger sisters and their best friends, Marina and Felicia. Back then, we had the figures to dress like supermodels, and we received a lot of attention from older male specimens. However, sooner or later, the fear of my mother kicked in, and I dashed their hopes with my sarcastic remarks.

My favorite school activities were public speaking and acting in the theater group. I became a prefect in my final year. (Prefects were invented by smart schoolteachers to help them catch out naughty pupils during lunch break, so that they could drink coffee and smoke cigarettes in the staff room.) We were given silly duties like catching out the talkers during assembly, making sure the girls' nails were short but not their dresses, and so on. I was the big fish in the small pond. I begged my father for days to allow me to go to prefects' camp, and after tears and a lot of begging, I managed to convince him that I would be safe. During camp we built our own houses out of logs in the magnificent mountains of the Eastern Transvaal. We had to sleep in our log houses, and we froze our butts off because it was the middle of winter, but it was a great adventure. The teachers taught us various leadership skills and made us play team-building games to lift our spirits.

In my final years at school I had the baffling task of deciding which career path I would follow. I wanted a job that would always be useful to people and that would never be replaced by the computer. I loved biology and found the human body fascinating. I also enjoyed working with people during my waitressing years. I decided to study something in the medical field. I remembered that our friendly family dentist had a lovely house and worked decent hours, so I decided to apply for dentistry at Wits University in Johannesburg. Dentistry was two years less than medicine; I thought I would save my father some tuition fees and save myself a few years of studying. My father thought that I was mad; he told me dentistry was a man's job and that I was supposed to get married and have a bunch of Cypriot children.

The very important end-of-year exams arrived, and after a lot of nail biting, soup bowls of coffee, studying, and praying, I passed with a high enough average to be accepted into dental school. My mother was very proud because I was making her dream of educating at least one of her children at university come true. For the final dance of the year, my mother used her designer sewing skills and made me a beautiful, black, fitted evening gown that had an open back and spread out at the bottom like a mermaid's tail. She patiently beaded hundreds of white pearls onto the straps and pearl flowers around the bust area. She also sewed elegant dresses for two of my school friends, Paulina and Jacqueline.

That Christmas my father sent us to Cape Town to visit **Theo** Savvas and his family. Cape Town is on the southern tip of South Africa, and from my uncle's house we had a view of the great Atlantic Ocean licking the feet of a large, godlike mountain. Even though it was summer, the air was breezy, and it was cooler than Johannesburg. Our hospitable uncle took us sightseeing. Our first stop was the famous Table Mountain, which we admired while standing on a golden beach. We drove to Sea Point, where the two oceans meet, and spotted whales swimming in the distance. We walked along Boulder's Beach alongside black-and-white penguins, and in the botanical gardens we saw glorious South African flora like the protea. As we left the parking lot, a sneaky baboon stole the bag of an unsuspecting Chinese tourist.

During another day trip, our generous uncle drove us an hour away to a breathtaking winery which was surrounded by hundreds of grapevines, in the town of Stellenbosch. My sister and I got slightly tipsy after tasting a few South African wines. Our smooth skinned Aunt Artemis showed us how to make homemade facial masks with strawberries and avocado, and she took us for scenic drives around winding mountains. We sang along to the romantic song "Sole Mio" which played on my aunt's car radio. We walked with our little cousins Eleni and Omeros along Muizenberg Beach, and we studied the stranded sea creatures and the foam that had washed up on the shore because of the violent waves. The ocean was icy cold, the currents were too rough for swimming, and the great white shark lurked somewhere in the distance, so we decided to watch the brave surfers instead. The day before we left, we helped my aunt make a Greek salad while my uncle barbecued a mouthwatering, red Roman fish that he had bought that morning from the local fishermen at the harbor. Naturally, my uncle had a bowl of olives on the lunch table. (A true Cypriot never forgets his olives.) That was the last time we went on holiday in South Africa. It was a wonderful break before my studies at university.

Chapter 5:

Acquiring the Knowledge to Make My Dreams Come True

I was very fortunate that my father could pay for my education at university. Those were fun, wonderful years but also very challenging and intense. In first year, only 5 percent of the class passed our first chemistry exam; alas, I was not one of them. It took me a while to learn how to study for university-level classes, and I went from getting distinctions in high school to being ecstatic even if I just passed. During the first few years of our studies, we had the same subjects as the medical students, as well as extra dental subjects in the afternoon. My favorite subject was anatomy. I loved learning about all the bones, muscles, arteries, nerves, and organs that we have in our body. I was amazed at how efficiently our organs work. God made us so complex. I realized how ridiculous racial discrimination is because beneath our differently colored skin, we all look exactly the same. It is not ethical for me to discuss the cadavers we had to study, but I am grateful to the people who donated their bodies to medicine so that we could have the opportunity to learn. One of the most challenging subjects, one which intensified my fear of germs and unseen things, was microbiology. Do you know how many diseases can be spread by kissing alone?

During my years at university, I formed great friendships with students of different religions and nationalities. I learned a lot from my new friends and will always have them in my heart, no matter how many years go by. South Africa is not called the rainbow nation for nothing, and our group of friends was like a pot of mixed spices.

My Israeli friend, Rina, taught me that Jewish people are not allowed to eat any crustaceans or pork; they only eat kosher meat, and they are not allowed to mix meat with dairy products. My humorous Indian friend, Shahana, taught me that Muslim people are not allowed to eat pork; they only eat halal meat, and they are forbidden to drink alcohol. She also taught me to eat chili sauce with my pizza. My Taiwanese friend, Kai, who is a Buddhist (or an atheist—he was not sure), told me that in his country, some people eat dogs and various insects and drink snake's blood. My beautiful Indian friend, Veerusha, taught me that for the Hindu people, the cow is sacred, so they are not allowed to eat beef, and in her country the cows roam the streets and are not disturbed. She also showed us an Indian dance where she moved her head from side to side like a hypnotized snake. An African friend told me that in his village, they eat big fat mopane worms, which they pick off a tree. (That was when I realized that the snails and sheep's brain that I had eaten were not that weird after all.) My Indian friend Vibha, a vegetarian, shared her roti with me and tried to convince me that soybeans taste just like meat. I told her, "In my family, there are no vegetarians... and good luck trying to convince a Cypriot to give up lamb." I drove to university with Vanessa, my Greek buddy from high school. She was responsible for my addiction to the TV series Friends, and she taught me how to laugh while eating a lot of chocolate. I tasted her mother's scrumptious Greek cooking when we were studying at her house. My brave friend Vanessa let me drive her mother's car in her neighborhood before I had my license—until the day that I drove it into a tree.

Our African friend, Quakoo, had the best build and he became our personal bodyguard when we went clubbing. Our smart, Cypriot friend Aphrodite was the party animal, our Yugoslavian friend, Vladimir, was the cute guy in the class that most of the girls had a crush on, and I better not tell you what our hilarious South African friend, Daryl, ate in anatomy class, for the sake of his wife and children. We studied hard and we partied hard; those were the joys of being a student. I felt very privileged when I was invited to attend my friends' Jewish, Muslim, and Hindu engagement parties and weddings. I experienced some of their wonderful traditions, and I tasted new, delicious foods.

The most unforgettable experience we had in medical school was watching a birth in the general hospital. The baby was born by caesarean section because the unfortunate mother had syphilis (a sexually transmitted disease) and the doctors did not want to infect the baby. It felt like watching a miracle when the doctor pulled out the tiny African baby, with his coarse peppercorn hair, and cut his umbilical cord. Unlike us, the mother of the baby was expressionless. We found out that she was only fifteen years old and had been raped in her township.

We learned about so many sexually transmitted diseases that today I get annoyed when I watch blockbuster movies that portray strangers having casual, unprotected sex as if it is the norm of modern society. During our training, we saw many cases of AIDS—and HIV-infected patients an eye-opening part of our studies. A lot of these patients were poor, uneducated women from the African townships. At that time, 70 percent of HIV-infected people lived in sub-Saharan Africa. We had to learn all the symptoms and signs that appear in the mouth of an immune-compromised patient. One in every four patients that we treated had HIV. One of my friends pricked herself twice with a dental needle after it had been in a patient's mouth, and because there was a concern about HIV, she had to take AZT medication twice, which had unpleasant side effects. During my studies I realized that many lives are lost because of poverty and lack of education. We learned to appreciate how fortunate we were growing up. We had a family that loved us and who could afford to provide us with housing, food, and an education.

To change the somber topic, I will reveal a funny incident that happened in dental school the one day. One of the students was cleaning a cavity in a patient's mouth when all of a sudden he started shouting, "I found a fat worm! There is a fat worm!" We were in awe as this was not something we had learned about. The surprised supervising professor went to have a look. "You idiot!" he shouted at the student. "This is not a worm. It is popcorn stuck in a hole!" The patient got up very frightened and ran away.

Our first tooth extraction was very dramatic. Our patient was an elderly lady who was chaperoned by her teenaged granddaughter. As one of the students confidently started pulling and pushing on the lady's molar with the forceps, we heard a loud thud. Someone had fallen on the floor. The professor in charge quickly surveyed the dental students, assuming one of us had fainted. It turned out that it was the lady's granddaughter; she fainted after seeing a little blood and hit her head on our dental light on the way down. We had to rush her to the emergency doctor because her head was bleeding. I remember only one incident when a student pulled out the wrong tooth. Most of the time, we did a fantastic job.

We had an outstanding university and excellent professors. Our final year at dental school descended on us like an eagle descending on its prey. We had finally learned how our complex body works, how many teeth we have in our mouths, how to drill and fill cavities, and how to extract a molar without killing our patients. I am very grateful to all those fearless patients that allowed us to practice in their mouths.

During our final year, we had to take part in some charity work. The dental students were allocated a week or two, to practice and reside on a train called the Phelopepa, which runs through the rural areas of South Africa. The train was fully equipped to offer free medical services to all the impoverished people in the towns near the train's route. On the train, there were dentists, doctors, psychologists, and optometrists. It was a humbling, spiritual experience. Every morning, starting before sunrise, hundreds of poor African people waited in queues, sometimes in the freezing cold. They were so grateful for the treatment we gave them that a few danced for us, and others cried tears of joy. I remember filling the teeth of an elderly African man who wore an antelope skin over his shirt. He told me that he was the local witchdoctor. I tried to explain to him that he needed a scale and polish to remove the tartar from his teeth. He laughed and told me that if he did that, his five wives would not want to kiss him anymore because the "stone" on his teeth made his mouth taste sweet. We had to teach the people how to brush and floss their teeth. Some of them did not have enough food to eat-let alone a toothbrush. We had to improvise and show them how to use a soft twig as a toothbrush, salt water for toothpaste, and the string from a potato sack as dental floss. I understood why St. Francis of Assisi once said, "For it is in giving that we receive." The appreciation we felt from those grateful patients was worth more than all the money in the world.

On the way back home from the Phelopepa train, my friends and I were packed like sardines in Kai's little car. There were seven of us with six different religions. We chatted and laughed during the long ride home. When it started to get dark, we decided to overtake the slow truck that was in front of us. All of a sudden we saw the lights of an oncoming car headed straight for us at what appeared to be lightning speed. There was no where for Kai to turn—on his left was the truck he overtook, and on his right there was a pavement. All seven of us automatically started praying. We prayed to God, to Jesus, to Allah, to Moses, to the Hindu gods, and I am pretty sure that atheist Kai prayed to Buddha. By some kind of miracle, a power took over Kai's hands, and he managed to overtake the truck and get us out of danger a split second before the oncoming car whizzed past us. Kai said he had no control of his hands.

I believe in the power of prayer. Whenever I am in trouble, I pray to God, and he always helps me in the way he knows is best. I am very thankful that my mother taught me how to pray. By her example, my maternal grandmother taught me to pray for good health, for protection from evil, for forgiveness, and to thank God daily for all of my blessings. I have learned to be very careful what I pray for and what I complain about. After moaning that my first car was not good enough for me, it was stolen while parked outside my university. God has taught me to be grateful for many things more than once in my life.

The only complaint I have from university is that we don't have a decent final-year class photo. The original pictures were lost when the photographer's car was stolen and, a day before graduation, we were told to gather all the students for a new photo; because it was rushed the scene was not very well organized and half the students' heads are hidden away!

Graduation day arrived, and I became the first person in our family to obtain a degree. My parents and relatives were very proud. I felt happy and relieved that I had passed, and I was ready to open the door of my future as a working adult.

Chapter 6:

Becoming an adult in Cyprus

y parents had waited for me to graduate so that they could sell our house. My father was fed up with the crime, and my mother's greatest wish was to return to her birthplace and spend time with her elderly parents. Eighteen years after we'd arrived as immigrants, we sold our beloved house in South Africa and returned to Cyprus with a container filled with oversized furniture (instead of a suitcase in our hands). Note to any South African immigrating to Cyprus: if you are not a millionaire leave your furniture behind, as Cypriot houses are a lot smaller. We felt sad and guilty to leave South Africa, the country that had filled our years with many good memories.

A few years before we left South Africa, I met my tall, extroverted husband, Nick. He was well built, handsome, and had these dark, piercing eyes that would stare into my soul. As the Greeks would say, it was my destiny or my prewritten luck to meet him. Nick's mother is Afrikaans, and his late father was born in Greece but grew up in South Africa. Nick was spiritual, passionate about Latin dancing, and quite the romantic. He asked me to dance salsa with him in a club one night, and that was the beginning of the end. He wrote me love letters, showered me with compliments, played romantic music, and told me all the things a girl wants to hear. He corrupted my innocent brain and made me fall in love (or lust—I am not sure). Nick did not believe me when I told him that I was still a virgin. Then he met my strict Cypriot mother. He waited many years before getting any action! (No, I will not write about all those details because this is not a romantic novel.)

Nick was not the ideal suitor that my parents would have chosen: he was not Cypriot, he barely spoke Greek, he had no degree, he had to work two jobs to pay his debt, he didn't drive a Ferrari like some of the Greek boys I had dated, and he was two heads taller than my father. Nick became the forbidden fruit, and so, from being the responsible child, I became the family rebel. Eventually my parents accepted the fact that stubborn Nick was not going to disappear, and they grew fond of him. My uncle Costa once told me that the most persistent man always gets the girl—as usual, he was right.

After two years of dating, Nick took me to his favorite little Greek church in Johannesburg called Saint Nektarios. Nick's official name is actually Nektarios as he was named after the saint. We did our usual routine: we lit our candles by the entrance and sat on a bench in the front row so that we could pray. The church was quiet and empty except for an old lady dressed in black, who was sitting at the back. Sunlight streamed through the windows, making patterns of light on the floor by my feet. After a while, Nick got down on one knee, pulled out a diamond ring, and, with a quivering voice, said, "I know that I don't have a lot of money, and I'm sorry I did not take you to an expensive restaurant, but I believe that the best things in life are free. I want to tell you in front of the eyes of God that I promise to always love you with all my heart and soul. Will you marry me?"

Tears poured down my face as if someone had turned on the tap behind my tear ducts. I was so shocked that I forgot to say yes until we got back to the car. During the drive back home, I felt overwhelmed by a sense of happiness and uncertainty, and I was afraid of my parents' reaction. I had just graduated, Nick was twenty-four and still living with his parents—what did we really know about life and marriage at that age? All I knew was that he had a good heart, came from a loving, close-knit family, and had saved all his hard-earned money to buy me a diamond ring. I later found out that Nick had asked my father's permission before he had proposed. My father must have been stunned. The last time someone had asked his permission was when an elderly African man saw me at his grocery store and offered him ten cows for my hand in marriage.

To Nick's dismay, a few months after he proposed, I moved to Cyprus with my family. At first we stayed with our beloved *Thea* Maria and Uncle Costa, who had returned to Cyprus before us and had built their own house. I remember my efficient Uncle Costa waking us up early every Saturday to help with spring cleaning of the house. Uncle Costa is the only man I know who can iron a shirt and make up a bed neater than a woman. After a few months, we rented a two bedroom apartment with my parents, and I shared a room with my youngest sister, Angela.

One hot summer evening as we were getting ready for bed, three cockroaches (that looked like they were on steroids) crawled into our room from the open window, as if to welcome us to our new home. Angela went berserk—she hates all insects with a passion; even tiny moths make her freak out. I had to hunt and kill the filthy creatures with my shoe to end my sister's panic attack. Angela was worried that more insects would crawl in through the window, so she grabbed a sheet out from the cupboard, wrapped it around herself like a cocoon, and stayed that way until the morning. I was surprised that she did not bake to death in the thirty-degree (Celsius) heat of summer!

After a few months of trying to get on my feet, I met my kindhearted, green eyed, third cousin Demetra. (Cypriots eventually meet all their second and third cousins.) Demetra, a real socialite, introduced me to many people. Besides being the queen of Scrabble, she is also a great cook and loved arranging dinner parties. She introduced me to my friends Maria and Elena, two beautiful sisters with dark eyes and hair as black as a raven's wing. We enjoyed eating out at the various multicultural restaurants in the town of Paphos; with this, my social life in Cyprus had started to sprout.

After ten months Nick followed me to Cyprus, because, he tells me, he loved me too much to lose me to some short Cypriot man. He left behind a loving family and a job in finance, in which he had just started to do well. Starting a new life on an island and in the small town of Paphos, which survives mainly on tourism, was a challenge to say the least. We were lucky that we had relatives and friends that shared their knowledge and guided us. Nick eventually found a job with a developer that sells homes to English expatriates. After the economic crisis spread to Cyprus, property sales declined and Nick decided to pursue his passion and become a professional photographer. The love he has for his work is expressed in his unique and creative photographs, and I have used many of his images in this book.

When I first arrived in Cyprus I went to several dental clinics looking for work, but to no avail. There are so many dentists and doctors for the population that competition is not welcomed with open arms. In Cyprus there is an abundance of degrees and not enough jobs because a Cypriot parent's greatest dream is educating his or her children. Money is saved from the time the child is born so that it can be used for the child's studies in the future.

I decided that if I could survive living in crime-ridden Johannesburg and passing dental school, a little island was not going to stop me from achieving my dreams. I learned that in this universe, and especially in Cyprus, it is not what you know but whom you know that gets you what you need. So, with the help of a family friend, I met Nitsa, a wonderful colleague who allowed me to work with her for a few months and treat my own patients in her clinic. I learned a lot from Nitsa's experience, and I will always be grateful for her trust. At that time I had no money to buy a car, so for a few months I had to walk to Nitsa's practice, even in the scorching heat of summer. (I was fifteen kilos lighter back then, so there are some benefits to being poor.)

My dream was to open my own practice, even though I was penniless and could not turn to my parents or struggling fiancé for financial help. The exchange rate between the South African rand and the Cypriot pound was ridiculous at that time. My parents had just managed to pay off the mortgage on our house in South Africa, and they were left with a pinch of profit. My parents sold our three-bedroom house in South Africa for 400,000 rand, which at that time was equivalent to 30,000 Cypriot pounds—that amount does not even buy a one-bedroom apartment in Cyprus. My parents had to apply for another mortgage, and they both had to look for work at an age when they should have been planning for their retirement. My father was hired as a gardener by a big developer. His work is backbreaking and exhausting in the heat of summer, but he carries on with it, because trees are his passion. My mother was thrilled to land a job at a big supermarket because it was her first job, and she would earn her own salary.

I once read a Swedish proverb that says: God gives every bird a worm, but he does not throw it into the nest. I was determined to catch my own worm. I have always believed that with the help of God, I can achieve anything I set my mind to. It all starts off with a spark of inspiration and an idea in my head—like the crazy idea to write this book. Once I have an idea, it attaches to my brain like a hungry octopus, and it doesn't let go until I have transformed it into my reality. I believe that after the age of 18, we can create our own financial luck in life, by making the right choices and grabbing every opportunity that comes our way. I admire people (like Oprah) that have faced many hardships in their lives but they still managed to make their dreams come true. In Cyprus, many people expect the government to solve their financial problems but that is very unrealistic.

I managed to convince a Cypriot bank manager (who looked at me as if I was a greedy *kalikantzaro* [gremlin] after his money) to grant me a loan. Of course, that was after I provided two signatures from two guarantors, a deposit of 5,000 Cypriot pounds that I borrowed, and one of my grandfather's pieces of land as security. The banks in Cyprus are some of the few in the world that didn't go bankrupt during the recent economic crisis because they have never granted loans for pleasure. When you live in a small town, to avoid being disgraced, you do not miss monthly loan payments—all the bank tellers recognize your face, know your first name, occupation, telephone number, physical address, and the personal details of your entire family. There is an amusing yet shocking saying amongst the locals that goes something like this: instead of losing your reputation, it is better to lose your eye!

My skeptical father worried that I would end up bankrupt. Uncle Costa spurred me on and told me to follow my dream. I rented a small shop and set up my own practice. After years of long working hours and trying my best to make my patients happy, I believe I have made it a success. For me the meaning of success is having the ability to help my loved ones, choosing my own working hours, and paying my bills at end of the month without having sleepless nights. I eventually bought the shop that I was renting and I transformed it into the practice of my dreams. My father's investment in my education has been paid back with free dental treatment—he now has the best-looking teeth in town! I am grateful to God and my family for all my achievements, and I appreciate everything I have.

Over the years, I have met many extraordinary people in my clinic, and many patients have become my friends. The first thing new patients ask me (after they share their horrible stories about how much they fear or hate the dentist) is whether I have heard that dentists have the highest suicide rate of all the professionals. I tell them that I find that very hard to believe, because, even though I have the ability to make grown men cry, my job is actually very rewarding. I did not become a dentist to hurt people; I became a dentist to help people. I must be doing something right, because a few kind and grateful patients have brought me gifts. I have received citrus fruit from their trees, honey from their hives, homegrown beans, olive oil, chocolates, oil paintings, flowers, books, wine, and handmade lace tablecloths. I even have a patient who brings me fresh eggs from his chicken pen every time he comes for his routine checkup. The only gift I need from my patients is a simple thank you and a smile because that is what makes my job worthwhile.

I love talking with my patients, and I have a terrible habit of asking them questions while I am busy digging in their mouths. My patients have also taught me many lessons over the years. One of the first things I learned from one of my English patients is that a traffic light is not called a robot (like it is in South Africa). I discovered this when I gave the patient directions to my practice, and I told him to turn right at the robot. The patient turned up an hour late and told me he drove up and down the street, looking for an android-like robot. My English patients are amused by my South African accent. My Cypriot patients are amused by my Greek accent. Greeks are amused by my Cypriot accent, and, if you are an American reader, you are probably amused by my English writing. I guess the world of language is an amusing place. As long as we all understand each other, who cares about dialect and grammar?

The one thing they forgot to teach us at university is how to run a business. I had to learn that on my own. I have learned the importance of good bookkeeping. I have learned that when I allow patients to owe me money, I usually never see them again. I try to help patients that genuinely cannot afford treatment, but I have to be cautious because

I have my own mountain of debt, and wretched money is a necessity! My new dream is to be debt free so that I can provide free treatment to any patient that needs it. I am still searching for my purpose in this life, and I know how rewarding it feels when you give back to the less fortunate. Every time I have done some good in my life, it has always come back to me tenfold.

I have learned that the most important thing that money can buy is precious family time. I have learned that the best form of advertising is word of mouth. I have learned that 98 percent of people appreciate what I do, but 2 percent will always be pessimists, no matter how hard I try to please them. I have learned that my education did not end at university, and that it is a lifelong process that has to be constantly updated. I have learned that dentistry is not an exact science. I have learned that there are many people in this world who have dental phobias, and I have to be extra gentle, play relaxing music, and take out my stress ball just to get some patients to sit in my chair. I have learned that children will always love sweets, just like I did as a child, so I teach them how to take care of their teeth because prevention is better than cure. And I have learned that as much as I try to convince them otherwise, some adults will only visit the dentist when they have an abscess the size of a tennis ball and are suffering from excruciating pain. I pray that all the treatment I provide will allow my patients to smile with pride, take away their dental pain, and preserve their teeth so that they can chew on glorious food as long as possible.

In the beginning of my career, I was the receptionist, the cleaner, the dentist, the oral hygienist, the assistant, and the bookkeeper. When my practice started to do well, I could finally employ some help. A wise uncle once told me that charity should begin at home, so I decided to help my family first. Surprisingly, it took a lot of persuasion to convince my mother to leave her job at the supermarket (which was less pay and longer working hours) and become my messenger and dental nurse. My youngest sister, Angela, worked as my receptionist for a few years until she got married and had an adorable baby boy called Dimitri. (He is on the book cover.) She decided it was more fun being a stay-at-home mommy than listening to patients' dental problems all day long. Also she gets to sleep late in the mornings—which has always been her greatest wish. (Angela now makes the best cupcakes.) Her hardworking husband, Andro, is also from Steni village, and our grandmothers are neighbors and good friends. They are the sweet grannies on the cover of this book, and they are holding baby Dimitri, their shared great-grandchild. I used their photograph on this cover because the love they have for their grandchildren captures the essence of my book.

With the help of my sister, I found another pretty and friendly receptionist, who is South African- Portuguese. Her name is Anna, and she is married to a South African-Cypriot. Anna is a hardworking, honest girl who writes a lot of notes, and at times she is my second brain. Without her, my dental practice would not run as efficiently as it does. She also makes delicious South African cakes. One day, a tall, blond, German girl with emerald-green eyes walked into my practice looking for work. Susanna is the most punctual person I have ever met, and she is an excellent oral hygienist—a real "Germinator." They really do make the most efficient machines in Germany. She is also our fitness muse. Every day Susanna eats at least five oranges, drinks two and a half liters of green tea, and does four hundred sit-ups, amongst other exercise—no exaggeration. She also makes the best pork schnitzel and apple crumble. Susanna calls me her "little Jamie Oliver" because I love experimenting with new recipes, and I often take my dishes to work for everyone to taste. The secret is out—all the women in our clinic love to eat. My employees have been a great help to both my practice and me, and I feel very blessed to have met them. We make a great team, and they have become part of the family.

On weekends, I enjoy walking, swimming in the summer, cooking, reading, and my most recent experiments, learning how to paint, ice-skate and play the Spanish guitar. My favorite hobby is entertaining my young nephews. My sister Dora moved to Cyprus three years before us. She met her Cypriot husband, Sotiris, got married, and settled in my mother's village of Steni. Sotiris comes from the village of Peristerona, which is found between my mother's village of Steni and my father's village of Lysos. He is fanatical about his ten hunting dogs, which get on my sister's nerves. (Hunting is the favorite sport of the macho Cypriot male.) Sotiris trains his hunting dogs to catch wild rabbits in the surrounding hills. He works for the electricity board during the week, and on weekends he runs a small clay-pigeon shooting range in the village of Lysos. (Many Cypriots have two jobs to survive the economic crisis.) Dora works full time for a stunning five-star hotel called Anassa, and she is also a fantastic cook. Have I mentioned that she is one of those annoyingly gifted people that can eat as much as they like and never gain weight, without doing a stitch of exercise? The fact that she has two active children and keeps the cleanest house in the village, without a maid, must contribute to her above mentioned gift. Her husband and eldest son never fail to take off their muddy boots before they enter their house. All the years of my mother's "good housewife" training rubbed off on all three of us, but especially on Dora. I felt very blessed when I baptized Dora's firstborn, Savvaki. It is a great honor to baptize a child in the Greek Orthodox Church. The godparents and parents share the responsibility of teaching the child about God and guiding the child's soul closer to heaven.

Should anything ever happen to the child's mother (God forbid), the godmother may help raise the child. The day of the baptism was very exciting for all our relatives. The only problem was that any baby being baptized usually cries a lot, and, to an outsider, the baptism ceremony must appear like a cruel torture session.

Guided by the priest, I had to face the west side of the church, which is the direction of evil. I had to read a prayer that praises God and rejects evil, and I had to spit on the devil (the floor). The priest that performs our family's church services is called **Papa** Theoris [Father Theodoros], and he is from my mother's village of Steni. (He has eight children and is the godfather of my sister Angela.) The priest told me it was time to undress the baby. The minute I started to undress three-month-old Savvaki, he started crying. The priest blessed some olive oil and anointed the baby's forehead, chest, shoulders, ears, hands, and feet, making the sign of the cross. This is done to give the baby the strength to fight the powers of evil in the world. The baby was then immersed in and lifted out of a copper font which was filled with warm water. The priest had earlier poured olive oil into the water in the shape of a cross. The baby was immersed three times in the name of the Father, the Son, and the Holy Spirit. The immersion is important in an Orthodox baptism because it follows the example set by Jesus at his baptism. By that stage, Savvaki was screaming his lungs out.

I had to hold a white sheet, which was spread over my shoulders, and Savvaki was put in my arms. The priest anointed the baby again with another holy oil that represents the gift of the Holy Spirit. The baby was dressed in the handsome baptism outfit that I had bought him, and a gold cross was put around his neck. Holding my godchild, I had to follow the priest around the baptismal table while holding a big gold cross. My youngest cousins, Maria and Yiannaki, held a large, burning candle and followed me around the table. The priest then cut a few pieces of hair from the baby's head as an offering to God. Savvaki was then given his first Holy Communion. During our baptisms, the mother is not allowed to touch her child, as much as it pains her to hear her baby crying. Only when the church service is over and the baby is a Christian does the priest then hand the child over to the mother.

Today my godchild calls me **nouna** (godmother), and I feel very special. I talk to him about God and have showed him how to pray. I hope that when he is older, he will remember some of the spiritual things I have taught him. I love all my nephews as if they were my own children. I pray that God will always keep them safe and healthy and keep them on the right path in their lives.

After seven years of being in our roller-coaster relationship (can't live with you, can't live without you), Nick and I decided to do the right thing, give in to the pressure from the relatives, and get married in the Greek Orthodox Church.

Three months before our wedding, my beloved *Pappou* Savvas was very ill in hospital. His arteries had clogged up from sixteen years of uncomfortable dialysis treatment. Unfortunately, he suffered from kidney failure just before he became a pensioner. The doctors said his kidneys could have failed because he did not urinate frequently enough when he was younger because he worked all day in the fields. It could have also been all the pesticides he used in the past. I went to visit my grandfather in the hospital, and it was heartbreaking to see him frail and in pain, with tubes coming out of his nose. All his children were by his side, weeping softly. His eyes were closed, and he was practically in a coma. We all thought it was his end. I bent down and told him to be strong, and to get better because I wanted him to dance at my wedding. I also told him that he was the kindest man I had ever known and that one day he would be in heaven. I was not sure if he could hear me.

The next day my grandfather surprisingly recovered from his comatose state and told the doctors that he did not want any more treatment. He simply wanted to go home. He had always praised the doctors and the nurses that had looked after him at the hospital during all the years of dialysis treatment. The nurses told my mother that he was the only man in the dialysis ward that never complained and always greeted them with a smile. I went to visit him at his home a few days later. He was in his bed, half asleep and very weak. When he saw it was me, he used the little strength that he had to whisper a blessing. He told me that he wished for us to always be happy, and he thanked me. I am not sure why he thanked me. Perhaps it was for the measly flower I had bought him or for the dental treatment I had given him when he was still able to walk. Perhaps he had heard the words I whispered in his ear at the hospital. Even though he was suffering and fighting off death, he told my grandmother to keep money aside for my wedding day. He was surrounded by all his children and grandchildren, and that was all he ever wanted out of his life. He was happiest when we were all together. He did so much for all of us, and we felt so helpless because we could not do anything to take away his pain.

According to our tradition, I had to spend the night before my wedding day, at my mother's house, apart from my soon-to-be husband. As I lay in the bed, I felt very nervous about my big day. Our relationship was nothing like those in the romantic American movies I had watched. I will not elaborate on our numerous issues because there are many people in this world with more severe problems than ours. I prayed hard for God's guidance and asked him if I was doing the right thing by getting married. After hours of stressful thoughts, tears and intense praying, the strangest thing happened to me. God decided to play a divine joke and a spiritual vision appeared before me. Unless somebody drugged my tea, I am pretty sure that it was not a dream, because my eyes were wide open and I was able to look around the room. I saw the wrinkled hand of an old man, which I assumed to be God's. This gentle hand took my hand and held it tight, and a soothing, manly voice told me that everything was going to be okay. At that moment, I felt very peaceful. It was a feeling that I had never felt before—as though the Holy Spirit had entered my soul. All my worries disappeared, and I fell into a deep relaxing sleep.

October 7, 2007, finally arrived, and my grandfather made it to our wedding day. He was in a wheelchair. Uncle Costa pushed the wheelchair to the front of the church so that my grandfather could see us better, while *Papa* Theoris (the priest) was placing the white wedding crowns on our heads. The crowning was done after the priest had exchanged our wedding bands, which were sitting snugly on our right hands. The priest switched our wedding crowns (which were joined together by a ribbon) back and forth and repeated a special blessing three times for each of us. The Greek wedding crowns are a visible reminder of the crowns that await us in heaven.

My handsome three-year-old godchild (and pageboy) wanted to push my grandfather's wheelchair. It is an image I will never forget. Savvaki (little Savvas) is my grandfather's first great-grandchild. Four generations of relatives were witnessing my marriage. When I saw them together, I noticed that there were tears streaming down my grandfather's cheeks. I am not sure what he was thinking at that time; I can only imagine. He knew he did not have long to live, and I feel that he was happy because he had made it to my wedding day. It was the most emotional day of my life. That image triggered my tears, which poured down my face throughout the rest of the ceremony. I cannot remember the priest's words because my mind was on my grandfather. Elena, my maid of honor, had to constantly wipe my face so that my makeup would not smudge.

The priest gave us his blessing and placed a piece of village bread in our mouths, which we had to chew and quickly swallow; it represented the body of Christ. We were then given sweet red wine to drink, which represents the blood of Christ. We followed the priest around an altar three times, followed by my maid of honor and the best man. The priest chanted a song from the Bible. At the end of the service, my husband and I bowed down so that our grandparents could kiss us on our heads and give us their blessings. At Greek weddings, we do not exchange vows; the wiser priest does all the talking. According to our tradition, I have hung my wedding crowns in a frame above my bed.

After our church service ended, my grandfather told my granny that he couldn't attend the dinner reception because he was weeping, and he didn't want to make anyone sad. When my grandfather was still healthy, he loved attending weddings and he would sit right in front of the dance floor to watch the traditional dancing.

My wedding day was a lot like the movie My Big Fat Greek Wedding, so I will not go into all the details. After a few short speeches from our drunken best man and my nervous husband, we ate and danced until the early hours of the morning. My wedding day ended too fast; all the months of stress and preparation were over in a few hours. At the end of the night, we retired to our hotel room and counted the money we received in the little white envelopes. Thankfully, there was just enough money to cover our wedding expenses.

The church service of a marriage in the Greek orthodox religion is amusingly called *to mystirio*, which means "the mystery." Marriage is definitely a great mystery. The Oxford English Dictionary defines mystery as "a matter that remains unexplained." Need I say more?

There are French and Arabian proverbs that say marriage is like a besieged castle; those who are on the outside wish to get in and those who are on the inside wish to get out. Whenever the squabbles of marriage test my patience, I try to remember the vision that God sent me before my wedding day. At times, I feel as though God is testing us to see if we have the guts to make it together until the end. In the meantime, he has a good laugh, eats his popcorn, and watches the trials and tribulations of the Love and Marriage Show.

The first thing I have learned in my marriage is that it takes a lot of compromise to keep two strangers living happily in the same house. I have learned how to forgive, and how to ask for forgiveness. I have learned that men do not change, no matter how much you try to change them. It has taken me years to accept the fact that my husband's taste buds are unadventurous—he will never eat snails, olives, cooked vegetables, or my *trahana* soup. I finally understand that no matter how many times I tell him, he will never put the new toilet paper roll on its proper dispenser. My father would often repeat this local saying, **o nouros tou shilou than ishoni**, which means a dog's tail does not straighten. My father likes to remind me that our ancestors fasted for 50 days before blurting out their wise quotes. They really knew what they were talking about! I am learning to love my energetic husband, with all his faults, and I pray that he is doing the same for me.

Another important lesson I have learned in my marriage is that female relatives are not psychologists, and marital squabbles are not meant to be shared. Cypriot women cannot keep secrets—it is like trying to keep a Jack in his box. In Cyprus people gossip about others to forget the scandals and problems in their own lives. The gossip usually passes via the broken telephone method, and by the time it reaches the neighbor's ears, it is a twisted, melodramatic version of the truth, with all the fancy trimmings required to make a best seller. The good thing about living in a small community that loves to gossip is that most citizens think twice before doing anything really bad.

As tricky as marriage can be, I would probably do it all over again (after drinking a few bottles of strong *zivania*). I still have a lot to learn about marriage but even though I am not an expert, my advice to the younger generation is: marry a person with good values who you respect and communicate well with; look at that person's bad habits and ask yourself if you can live with those habits for the rest of your life. Unlike our Cypriot grandmothers, we have the luxury of choosing our own partner in life, and yet the divorce rate in Cyprus is higher than ever. I think it is because the role of men and women has changed exponentially since my *yiayia's* maiden days. Today, women focus more on their careers, we pay bills, we cook and do the housework, we give birth and take care of the kids, and we have the pressure from magazine covers to keep slim and look fabulous at all times. We have become "superwomen" with nerves of steel and smooth, hair-free legs. Very few members of the male species have evolved enough to keep up with us, and the majority of men's egos have been hurt in the process. The problems of married couples are too complicated for me to solve, so I will not ponder that topic any longer.

During our wedding ceremony, my parents-in-law were sitting on our right side in the church. My tall, blue-eyed father-in-law looked very proud to see his son getting married. The light in the church was shining on his wavy, white-blond hair, and it made him look handsome and almost angelic. Sadly, that week was the last time Nick and I would see him. He passed away suddenly from leukemia at the age of fifty-seven a few months after our wedding. He had big dreams for the future. He was a good family man and spent a lot of quality time with his children. He was very much in love with his wife, and, unlike most Greek men his age, he was not afraid to show it. They loved to dance together, and at my wedding they were the envy of the crowd.

My loving grandfather passed away in his bed a few weeks after our wedding, and his suffering finally ended. My grandmother sat next to his body all night long and cried her heart out. Next to his body, she placed a clay bowl of olive oil, which the priest later poured in the shape of a cross over his burial site. Our dead bodies are anointed with the olive oil, just like we are anointed at our baptism. Unfortunately, the cemetery in Steni village is running out of space, so my grandfather was buried in the same grave site as of one his relatives. The bones of the long deceased relative were placed aside to make space for a new coffin. My grandfather was buried facing the east, which is the direction of light. A Christian death means eternal life with Christ, so the relatives tried not to wail too loudly. My grandmother threw pieces of village bread and koliva (boiled wheat grains mixed with almonds, sesame seeds, and pomegranate) on top of the soil that was thrown over the coffin. This is an offering to the birds so that the body's soul can be forgiven. We then lit candles and an oil lantern at the burial site; this symbolizes the passing of the person from darkness to the true light of Jesus.

After a depressing funeral service, we gave village bread and salty olives to the people present at the burial site because that is the tradition. We then walked to my granny's house, where we ate salty snacks like spinach and olive pies that were brought by some of the relatives. A window was kept open and an oil lantern was kept alight for forty days in the room where my grandfather passed away. We believe that after someone dies, the soul roams the earth for forty days visiting relatives and the house in which he or she lived.

Three days after my grandfather died, my aunt Maria told us that she smelled incense in her house, and she believes it was my grandfather's presence. I have no doubt that he is in heaven. Cypriots can be very superstitious and they have various rituals that get rid of peoples' phobias or that are meant to bring luck to a home. For example, the cry or sudden presence of an owl is supposed to be a bad omen that foretells a death in the family. I am not superstitious at all, but a day before my grandfather's death, a large owl swooped past my sister's car as we drove away from his home in the village, and one night before my father-in-law's death, I spotted a white owl perched on the electrical wires above my house. Was it pure coincidence?

My husband and I have been so busy launching our careers, and making excuses, that we have not put enough effort into having children. *Yiayia* Theodora is constantly praying to the Virgin Mary and all the saints for me to fall pregnant—she has even given me holy olive oil from the church of Saint Raphael to rub on my belly. My grandmother has complete faith that this will help. Even though she struggles to solve a puzzle designed for a five-year-old, she knows by heart all the prayers and the names of all the saints in her Greek Orthodox Bible. In our faith, we believe that the saints pray to God on behalf of the faithful. If we have not inherited the names of our grandparents, we are usually named after a saint. We celebrate our name day every year on the day allocated to our saint. Relatives may forget your birthday but they never forget your name day. There are so many similar names and surnames in Cyprus that when a traffic officer stops us on the side of the road, he asks the name of our mother and father just to make sure that the speeding fine will land at the correct address.

Thea Vathoulla (my mother's youngest sister), and her husband could not conceive for ten years. They visited many doctors, but when the medical treatments failed to make a difference, my aunt turned to God and became more religious. She read the biography of the miracle worker Saint Dimitri, and she prayed every night for forty days for the saint's help. After forty days, my aunt had three dreams of the saint, with his white beard and long white robe. One night she dreamed that the saint visited her house and gave their home a blessing. The second night, she dreamed that she was in a church and the saint gave her bread to eat, which we usually get at Holy Communion because it represents the body of Christ. The third night, my aunt dreamed that the saint gave her two injections into her belly and that the Virgin Mary covered her sleeping body with a blanket. My aunt awoke the next morning with pain in her abdomen, but she did not think anything of it and ignored her dreams. When my aunt missed her period that month, she went to see her doctor. She was ecstatic when the doctor told her that she was finally pregnant—and her faith in the saints increased. *Thea* Vathoulla's firstborn son is called Dimitri, after the saint.

As I get older and lose more of my precious hair, I am wondering if a successful career is enough to feel content with life. My sisters' lives are happier and more meaningful now that they have children. There is nothing more heartwarming and pure in this world than a baby's smile and laughter. If it is God's will, my grandmother's prayers will come true and we will have a baby of our own. In the meantime, the love I receive from my sisters' children is enough to silence all of my broody instincts. I love to see the wonder in my nephews' eyes when they see insects and animals for the very first time, and their facial expressions when they taste new foods. My godchild is six years old and he already loves Chinese food and sushi. I was seventeen the first time I ate at a Chinese restaurant, and I only tasted (and became addicted to) sushi in my twenties.

Chapter 7:

My Travels...Living My Dream

I f you hate reading travelogues then you should skip to the next chapter and I won't blame you. I added this chapter because my travels are a realization of my childhood dream, and by sharing my adventures I hope to inspire others to turn their dreams into a reality.

The best part about being a working woman is that I can save money for travel and I thank the men that invented the airplane. I have caught the highly contagious travel bug, and I don't believe there is a cure. Travel makes life feel extraordinary and helps me stay sane by allowing me to escape from work and the stress of everyday life. I believe that every country in the world has hidden wonders that are worth discovering. Why else have people from all the countries of the world fought so many wars to keep their land? When you live in a tiny town on a small island, you have to travel to realize how insignificant a human being is in this big, wide world. In our town we are recognized everywhere we go, and at times we feel a bit claustrophobic or like a celebrity longing to find anonymity.

Unlike my closed-minded father, I want to see as much of the world as I can before the angel of death comes to take my last breath. The only things we take with us when we leave this earth are our memories. When I ask my father why he does not like to travel, he tells me that he can see the whole world from his television set. I have offered to take him on holiday many times, but he tells me he would rather be tortured. Even driving an hour away to the next city is a huge mission for my father. He believes that his village in Cyprus and South Africa are the most beautiful places in the world, and he is not interested in seeing other lands. Hopefully I will manage to change his mind one day.

The Middle East and North Africa

Egypt

The first holiday I ever paid for with my own hard earned money was a cheap three-day cruise to Egypt. It was the summer of 2003 and I was accompanied by my optimistic friend, Elena. (After Maria, Elena must be the second most popular name in Cyprus). It was the first time either of us had been on a ship, and we enjoyed every minute, despite spending a lot of time in the toilet being seasick. We disembarked at Port Said, and, after a three hour bus ride through the chaotic roads of Cairo, we reached the desert. I was surprised that it was so close to the densely populated city. We were dumbstruck when we saw the enormous size of the ancient pyramids that were sitting like sunbathers in the golden sand. While we were there, we had to hide from a few Arab men that were following us, begging us to buy their Egyptian souvenirs. Back then we had no money to spare on trinkets. To escape, we decided to enter one of the pyramids, so we joined the queue of tourists. We had to hunch over because the tunnel entrance was only one meter high. Once we got to the end of the tunnel, where we could stand up straight, we were dripping wet from sweating in the heat. We expected to find gold and a mummy but we were told they had been taken to the museum. The tour guide then took us to see thousands of precious artifacts and mummies in the impressive Egyptian Museum. We also went to a papyrus factory, where we learned how papyrus paper is made.

I have also traveled to Sharm el-Sheikh, which is found in the south of Egypt, with my husband. It used to be a remote Bedouin fishing village, but it has now become a popular diving destination. The sea life we saw in the Red Sea was incredible. We snorkeled for hours admiring the different colored coral and fish of all sizes. I studied a huge, leopard spotted eel while it was swimming in and out of the sea rocks. At one stage my husband told me that he had found some anemone fish and I eagerly swam behind him in search of little Nemo, but I regretted my decision when Nick led us straight into a swarm of harmless jellyfish. I was stung several times before I decided to give up on Nemo and head for the shore as fast as I could. I was scolded by a furious, red-faced lifeguard because, in my haste to get out of the sea, I swam over the prohibited reef. On my way out, I almost stepped on a poisonous, spotted blue stingray that was hiding in the sand in the shallow water.

In the evenings, we savored warm Egyptian bread with spicy meals that woke up our dormant taste buds, and for dessert we ate super sweet dates. I also tasted the lotus fruit for the very first time, which is a seedy fruit that looks like an orange-red tomato but tastes very sweet when it is ripe. We drank Arabic coffee in the town square and smoked hubble-bubbles while we watched young Arabic men dance in the streets with their traditional white attire.

Israel

In 2005, I traveled to Israel to visit my university friend Rina. She showed me the city of Tel Aviv, and we walked through the old city of Jaffa. We ate tasty Israeli specialties like falafel, hummus, and bagels. We floated in the salty Dead Sea and rubbed mud all over our bodies, which made our skin feel so smooth that the goddess Aphrodite would have been jealous. That same day we also hiked for two hours through semiarid mountains until we reached the waterfalls of Ein Gedi. My fancy slippers broke on the way back, and I was forced to walk barefoot for one hour on hot, arid sand. (Serves me right for not taking hiking boots with me; back then I wanted to look glamorous at all times.)

We awoke our religious souls when we visited the Holy Land in Jerusalem. I watched as my Jewish friend wrote a prayer to God on a piece of paper that she folded many times and pushed into a crack in the Wailing Wall. I lit a candle and said my prayer in the nearby Christian church of the Holy Sepulchre, which was built on the spot where Jesus was crucified. We also admired the Muslim mosque with its golden dome, which is found a few steps away from the Christian church.

I was saddened when I learned that in such a holy place there is a lot of fighting and bloodshed over land. The three biggest religions in the world—Christianity, Islam, and Judaism—all have their roots in the same small piece of land, yet they are not united. Hopefully the day will come when the leaders of the world will find a peaceful solution for Israel and Cyprus. A year later, while attending a dental course, I drove to the Palestinian side of Israel with some colleagues to visit the isolated Greek Orthodox monastery of Saint Gerasimos. He was a priest who lived as a hermit in the desert and befriended a lion by taking a thorn out of its paw. The elderly nun and the young monk who take care of the monastery were very happy to see us, and they welcomed us with Greek coffee and local fruit. The monk asked me to stay behind and help out with the monastery, but I kindly refused.

Dubai

In 2007, I traveled with my sister Angela and my mother to Dubai, which is on the Arabian Peninsula and not far from Cyprus. Before the plane landed, we looked out the window and saw the unusual shapes of the man-made islands scattered in the sea. The ability of man to create never ceases to impress me.

When we landed at the huge airport, there was no taxi waiting for us as the travel agent had promised. We found our own taxi, and we were dropped off at our hotel, only to discover that there had been a mix-up, and we did not even have a booking. By that stage, my paranoid mother was in a panic. Eventually the corresponding travel agent in Dubai found us accommodation in a fabulous four-star hotel. The apologetic agent also gave us a gift of a free desert safari to apologize for their blunder. Dubai is one of the most buzzing, cosmopolitan cities I have ever seen. We saw many modern buildings and hotels, probably as tall as the tower of Babel from the Bible, reaching for the clouds. It is unbelievable how wealthy and developed a desert area became after the discovery of oil. Before that, the Arabs of Dubai traded spices, fabric, and dates with their neighbors, and they fished for oysters in the sea.

The desert safari was exhilarating. We went dune bashing for an hour through golden-brown desert sand in a white jeep with a driver who must have been insane. Our frightened mother told us that her heart was going to stop—every time her head hit the roof of the jeep. My sister and I loved the adrenaline rush. We were taken to a tent in the middle of the desert, where we sat on red cushions on the floor and ate various spicy foods while watching the seductive moves of a belly dancer. We held a tamed falcon in our hands, and we went for a bumpy ride on a camel. A dark-skinned woman with chocolate brown eyes who had her face covered with a black beaded scarf decorated our hands with temporary henna ink.

The following morning, after feasting on the breakfast buffet at our hotel, we walked to the down town market and golden souk. The sparkling yellow gold from the shop windows was hypnotizing. The air smelled of spice and perfume, and we were offered sweet Arabic treats by the stall vendors. During our shopping expeditions we got lost in massive shopping malls that seemed to have no end. One of the malls even had a big snow dome inside, with real snow, for the locals who are sick of the desert sand and long for a bit of skiing. My mother enjoyed Dubai, and I realized that she had contracted my travel bug.

The Indian Ocean

Seychelles

After a two and a half hour drive from Paphos, we arrived at Larnaca airport feeling very hot and annoyed. We had various arguments en route over whose fault it was for being so late for our flight. We entered the airport parking only to be told by the security guard that the employees were on strike. They refused to open the entrance boom so my angry husband decided to ignore them and drive over the pavement anyway. After parking, we ran inside with our large luggage bags and stood right at the back of the long queue. After forty minutes of waiting we were at the front desk. My tall husband gave the lady at the counter our passports, and his biggest smile, while he proceeded to request his list of: an aisle seat, extra leg room, in front, by an exit door, and if possible a window seat for his wife. The Emirates lady smiled back at him and said, 'Yes sir, your requests may be granted but the problem is your departure flight is for tomorrow afternoon at the same time!' During the long, two and a half hour drive back to Paphos, we argued about whose fault it was for not checking our departure date. (I still blame my husband because even though I booked the flight, he was the one that collected the tickets!)

Eventually we got it right and after landing in the Seychelles, we were taken by boat to the paradise island in the Indian Ocean called Silhouette. We call it the Garden of Eden because it was pure, unspoiled nature. Imagine large, black boulders sitting on white sand that overlooked turquoise waters and were surrounded by tall palm trees, with a lush green forest in the background. Our hotel was the only development on the entire island, and it was composed of wooden, thatch-roofed villas that were just a few steps away from the sea. On our first day, we sat on a white linen hammock in our private garden, admired our view, and thanked God for our blessings. Mangrove trees separated our villa from the neighbors on either side. To Nick's delight, we slept on a king-sized bed. Our spacious bathroom was surrounded by clear glass instead of curtains, so we had a view of the tropical trees that made up the backyard. After two days of romance, we were very bored with each other.

Instead of pampering ourselves in the hotel spa like the rest of the honeymooners, we decided to try scuba diving for the first time. Our bubbly French instructor was unusually tall and thin, and he had long, curly hair. He was confident as a teacher and showed us how to use our equipment in the hotel pool. When he thought we were ready, we were taken to the middle of the ocean and told to jump in. It took me a while to descend because my ears hurt, and I had to stop often to equalize. It was tricky trying to equalize by blowing out my nose, while breathing in the precious oxygen at the same time, but I kept reminding myself of the instructor's words: "If you stop breathing, you will die!" My husband and so-called diving buddy was already at the bottom exploring the sea life. When my ears were finally pain free, I reached the rest of the group below. When we were all confident, the fearless instructor guided us twenty meters below the surface of the sea. It was fascinating to see some of God's diverse underwater creatures. Our instructor picked up a sea worm, squished it with his hands, and long, luminous filaments squirted out. He made a warning hand signal when he saw a poisonous lionfish, and he annoyed an octopus that retaliated by squirting ink at him before swimming off. We swam with colorful parrot fish that had painted lips that looked like beaks. It was a blessing exploring the sea life on the ocean floor. We loved it so much that we went for a second dive.

We also hiked around the island with a guide and saw giant tortoises that my tall husband could sit on. The giant tortoise looked like it belonged to the dinosaur age. We spotted bright-green lizards and snails with massive shells amongst the plants. The guide pointed out the different tropical and rain forest trees that were planted by the French settlers. I was captivated by an extraordinary palm tree called the Coco de Mer; it has large seeds that physically resemble human female and male genitalia. The birds play cupid and take spores from the "male" seed to fertilize the "female" seed to produce a new tree.

When the stars were out, we watched crabs crawl in and out of shells on the beach, as if they were shopping for a bigger home. We sipped watery coconut juice out of a fresh coconut and tasted divine Creole food at the restaurants of the hotel. I tried not to disturb the spinning local dancers, with their tangerine- colored skirts, while I noisily cracked my lobster tail open with the provided utensil. I love lobster, and I must have eaten it four nights in a row because in Cyprus lobsters are scarce, too small, or ridiculously overpriced. For dessert we enjoyed sweet tropical fruit like papaya and mango. On our last day, we boarded the hotel ferry to visit the mainland. We shopped at the local market and watched as large, white seabirds tried to steal fish from the fishermen's tables.

Europe

Greece

Thanks to my husband's Greek roots, I have been very fortunate to explore a small part of mainland Greece and a few picturesque Greek islands. The marvelous history, mythology, and culture of Greece instill an egotistical pride in every Greek man's soul.

Athens

During my first visit to Athens we explored the mystical ruins of the

Acropolis and Parthenon, and I wondered which muse inspired the intelligent architects of ancient Greece. The speed of the underground metro impressed me since there are no trains in Cyprus. We strolled through Monastiraki, the famous flea market of Athens, shopping for souvenirs. We drank coffee on top of the hill of Likavitos, near the big church, and admired the view of the densely populated city of Athens.

I love Greek food, no matter what the American food critic Jeffrey Steingarten says in chapter 1 of his book *The Man Who Ate Everything*. How can he be the man who ate everything if he refuses to eat Greek food? Either he was bullied by a Greek classmate in school or he ate at some really bad Greek restaurants in his neighborhood. He should travel to Athens and ask the locals where he can eat the best freshly baked *tiropita* [cheese pie] or tastiest *gyro* shavings of slow-roasted, aromatic pork or chicken with crispy potato chips and *tzantziki* [a mixture of yogurt, garlic, lemon, salt, and mint] all served together on pita bread that has been grilled with a little olive oil. He should visit Nick's beloved grandmother, Maria, who lives just outside Athens and prepares delicious, home-cooked meals every time we go for a visit. For dessert he should have tea with Ero (our best man's wife), who makes the best *melomakarona* [orange and cinnamon flavored biscuits that are coated with honey and nuts] that I have ever tasted. (I'm pleased to say that she shared her secret recipe with me; see the last chapter.)

Ioannina

One Christmas holiday, we went on a six-hour drive with Nick's grandmother, exploring the western part of Greece. The time flew rather quickly because Nick's granny told us her entire life's story until we reached the town of Ioannina. On the way, we passed massive mountains and sparkling streams and rivers. Ioannina surrounds a famous lake, which has an interesting history involving the ruthless Ottoman Turk, Ali Pacha. Parts of Greece were under Turkish occupation for 400 years. When he invaded Ioannina, Ali Pacha went around the town and kidnapped the most beautiful Greek women for his harem. The women who refused him were tied up and thrown into the lake by his slaves. Frightened that he would be assassinated by his enemies, Ali Pacha had a secret getaway house built on a small island in the middle of the lake. Eventually his enemies found him, shot him from below while he sat on his wooden floor smoking his hubble-bubble, and beheaded him. The Greek slave girl that he had with him on the island was set free. We visited the island by boat and were greeted by the local shop vendors with sweet homemade liqueurs that helped to warm us up in the cold. In loannina's town square we drank *frappe* [frothy cold coffee with milk and sugar] and tasted their famous *bogatsa* (a sweet custard-filled pastry sprinkled with icing sugar). My husband ate *baklava*, his favorite Greek sweet.

In a nearby mountain village, we walked over an old cobbled bridge that crossed a river. We admired an outdoor "washing machine" that is powered by water that comes from the snow-capped mountain peaks. The water is led into two big wooden barrels, and it swirls around with a great force. In the springtime, the ladies from the village take their bulky sheepskin carpets to be washed in these barrels that do not require any soap. They then hang them on some nearby tree branches to dry.

We explored a large cave that extends for miles under a hill. The stalagmites and stalactites were magnificent. A few looked like giant, melted wax candles; a stalagmite not too far from the cave's entrance is shaped like a thick cross and is considered to be a miracle by the locals. On the way back to Athens, we stopped at a fish farm to buy some fresh trout for the relatives. We made a stop to eat our own sweet, fried trout in a restaurant along the way and sipped on a tot of ouzo, after toasting with the words *"Stin iyea sas,"* which means "to your health."

Zakynthos

During the summer of 2006, my husband and I flew to Zakynthos (also known as Zante), which is one of the seven Ionian islands. We traveled by ferry to an old shipwreck on a remote beach. All the pebbles on the beach were pure white, and it made the sea appear to be a milky blue. On the way back, we saw the bumpy Caretta caretta turtle peeking out from the sea. We were dropped off at the harbor, where we watched the Greek fishermen arrive with a huge, freshly caught swordfish. In the square, we studied a sleeping priest with a long white beard as he sat in the shade of a giant tree. We rented a car and drove around the whole island in a few hours. We stopped at a fish tavern to eat grilled octopus that was drizzled with olive oil and lemon. Another day, we stopped at a small restaurant to eat crispy suckling pig that was slow cooked on a spit on the side of the road. We swam in a private lagoon with crystal-clear water, and we walked on long stretches of sandy beach. We danced to Greek music in the clubs until the early hours of the morning. We visited Tuscan colored church towers in the mountains and went for a romantic ride on a horse-drawn carriage. The night before we left, we ate delicious, locally made ice cream on top of a hill under the stars; from that vantage point, we admired the lights of the town below us.

Rhodes and Symi

On my second three-day cruise, we visited the Greek island of Rhodes with my sister Dora, her husband Sotiris and her sister-in-law Andri. Because of rough seas, most of the passengers were seasick. I felt perfectly fine and was probably the only one on board that tasted all the food at the buffet tables - nothing gets in the way of my appetite. When the ship entered the port of Rhodes, we were greeted by a huge Byzantine castle. A tour guide took us on an excursion, and we walked through a fairy-tale forest that followed a stream. The trees were covered with ugly brown moths that were magically transformed into beautiful orange-colored butterflies, when they were startled and opened their wings to fly away. That evening, our cruise ship left Rhodes and headed for the neighboring island of Symi. The next morning, when we peeped out our cabin windows, we were pleasantly surprised to see rows of pretty, multicolored houses facing the sea. We bought silky soft sea sponges from the local fishermen, who told us that the first free divers in the world were Greek sponge divers.

Santorini

In 2010, I explored the Greek island of Santorini with my soft spoken, South African friend Maria (yes, another Maria). Santorini is part of the Cyclades islands. When we landed at the airport, we were greeted by a life-sized plastic donkey with the sign TAXI on its back. A real taxi then drove us to our charming hotel in the village of Oia. Hundreds of white, dome-shaped little houses with blue doors and window shutters were scattered on the cliff above the deep blue sea. White churches with blue-painted domes, big brass bells, and white crosses were found on every corner. Bright pink bougainvillea spilled over clay pots and splattered the white walls with color.

Traditional white windmills decorated a cliff edge. I had to pinch myself to make sure we were not living in a Greek postcard. We stayed in our very own cave house, and a delicious Greek breakfast of yogurt, cheese, honey, fruit, eggs, and bread was brought to our balcony every morning. We satisfied our hunger while admiring the stunning view of the sea. We fed our leftover breakfast to our daily visitor-a pitchblack cat that climbed over the snow-white walls of the neighboring houses to visit our balcony.

In the evenings we walked through the cobbled streets and admired the exquisite handmade art at the various galleries, which included sculptures of mermaids, seahorses, and swordfish made with golden brass, mirrors, and green stained glass. At the local taverns, we ate charcoal-grilled calamari kebabs and stuffed squid. We dipped warm pita bread into various tasty dips like *tzantziki*, and we munched on crispy salad, smooth feta cheese, and sweet, black Calamata olives. One morning, we decided to end our curiosity and descend hundreds of steps to see what was found at the bottom. We dodged a lot of donkey poop on the way down. When we finally reached the bottom, we found an enclosed beach, which was scattered with burnt-red and pitch-black pebbles. We drank a much-deserved *frappe* at a little tavern near the shore, and we had a dip in the sea to cool down. We managed to survive the long climb back up the steps, which could make the fittest marathon runner break into a sweat. The following day we went on a ferry excursion to visit the dormant volcanic island called Nea Kameni, which means newly burnt. It is found in the middle of the sea and is surrounded by the main land of Santorini. We hiked for two hours with a guide, exploring the charcoal-black volcanic hills, stopping only to observe the smoke that was blowing out of some holes. It resembled the surface of a distant planet. The last volcanic eruption took place fifty years ago, and we tried to step gently so as not to awake it.

England

In 2004, I flew to the United Kingdom to visit my Greek, school friend Vanessa, who now lives in the seaside town of Brighton. We traveled by train to visit London, which I had heard so much about from my English patients. I found the aristocratic architecture of the buildings very attractive. Like typical tourists, we snapped photos with Nelson Mandela, the queen of England, Madonna, and Makarios, the first president of Cyprus, in Madame Tussaud's Wax Museum. Being a woman, I was enthralled by the abundant stores on Oxford Street—it is a good thing for my pocket that shopping malls are scarce in Cyprus. My friend pointed out Buckingham Palace and the famous Big Ben. I felt like a real city girl when we saw the show *Chicago* at a London theater. On the way back to the station, all of our senses were brought to life when we got soaked in the rain—I finally understood why the English expats are always complaining about the British weather. I admired the fancy black London cabs, the red double-decker buses, and the old red telephone booths. We walked through a vast green park, and I was thrilled when I spotted a squirrel. (The English travel all the way to Africa to see the wild animals, but I almost wet my pants when I spotted a squirrel.)

I have since returned to London to attend dental seminars and courses. On one visit, my sister Angela, our friend Elpitha, and my mother came along for a bit of Christmas shopping and sightseeing. We walked for hours in many museums. Our favorite was the Natural History Museum, where we saw real dinosaur bones for the first time, amazing crystals, and ancient fossils. My mother was under the impression that dinosaurs only existed in the movies. We met up with Toulla, Angela's sister-in-law who worked in London at the time, and she gave us a tour of the Tate Modern Art Museum, London Bridge, and a wonderful food market, where we tasted different types of cheese and sausages.

During our trip, we also ate scrumptious English pies and delicious, freshly made soups at the buzzing Underground stations. The variety of treats and foodstuffs from all over the world that are sold in stores like Harrods and Selfridges is out of this world. I could not believe my luck when I found a packet of mopane worms on a shelf near the Selfridges food court. My excitement subsided later that evening when I took a bite of a worm and discovered that it tastes just like dried-up, salty leaves. However, the black pudding I ate at breakfast the next morning was even worse than the worm. I have this inexplicable belief that I should taste everything at least once in order to feel like I have truly lived.

We walked for hours down Oxford Street and admired the bright Christmas lights that adorned the shop windows and street lamps. We also got a glimpse of the bubbly nightlife of London as we walked past many pubs; my mother gave her disapproving look to a few drunken men who staggered out into the streets. Our hygienic friend Elpitha, who has an even greater phobia of germs than my whole family put together, was constantly disinfecting her hands after everything she touched, especially in the trains and subway stations—ironically, she is always the first to pick up all the bugs!

Austria and Hungary

In 2009, we toured Austria and Hungary with my mother, her shy cousin Stella, and a very enthusiastic Greek-Cypriot tour group. During the long bus drive to Vienna, we passed acres of bright-yellow sunflower fields. We noticed that there were no irrigation pipes in their crop fields, unlike those in Cyprus. In those parts of Europe, God waters the crops all year round. Our first stop was Schonbrunn Palace, the first palace we had ever seen up close. We were astonished by the rich details of the rooms where the royal family lived four hundred years ago. The palace fountains, gardens, and maze of trees were equally magnificent. I wondered what my humble *yiayia* Theodora would think of the palace. I don't think her mind can comprehend that so many years ago there were aristocrats that grew up in an atmosphere of complete luxury and wealth, while her parents and grandparents were poor farmers. We listened intently as the tour guide repeated the love story of Princess Sissi, the Hungarian princess who married her cousin, the king of Austria, at the age of sixteen. We learned about Mozart, the famous composer who began composing at a very young age and performed for the king, and we were impressed by Vienna's talented artists and painters from the Renaisance. My favorite painter was Ferdinand Georg Waldmuller; his paintings were so realistic that we thought we were looking at photographs. The Baroque grandeur of the fountains, buildings, and churches was aweinspiring. I found the Austrian food to be more simplistic than their historical buildings, while we dined on Austrian sausages, crispy chicken schnitzel, and apple strudel. We bought fresh berries and cherries from the fruit market, and savored them while walking through a marvelous green park.

In Hungary, we admired more grand Baroque buildings and bridges, while we sailed on a ferry down the brown Danube River. During our last evening, we went to a traditional Hungarian restaurant, where we watched Hungarian dancing and ate a hearty goulash stew, which is beef pieces slow cooked with chopped tomatoes, onions, garlic, bay leaves, potatoes, and red spices like paprika and cayenne pepper. (In Greece they add red wine and cinnamon and call it *kokkinisto*.) In the famous shopping street of the old city I bought a Hungarian secret box that amuses my guests for hours when they try to open it.

Italy

What does a woman do when she needs a break from a very stressful period in her marriage? If you have read Elizabeth Gilbert's novel *Eat, Pray, Love*, you will know that the correct answer to that question is: "she flies to Italy." In my case, accompanied by my sister Dora. During the entire four-hour flight from Cyprus to Rome, tears flowed from my tear ducts like a burst pipe; my sister and the unfortunate stranger who sat to my right tried their best to console me. When we landed at the airport, I swallowed my grief when my big-sister instinct kicked in and I had to find an honest taxi driver to drive us safely to our hotel. We were dropped off in a cobbled street of the town Trastevere, which is a fifteen-minute walk from Rome. When I stepped foot on the cobbled streets, I became aware that I had packed two pairs of heels in vain, and they would just be taking up valuable shopping space in my suitcase.

Our traditional Italian hotel was a renovated four hundred-year-old monastery that was adorned with many religious paintings and frescoes. It even had its own Catholic church, where the nuns said their prayers every morning. The shy nuns that walked briskly through the hallways were responsible for cleaning the rooms, which were immaculate. From the window of our hotel room, we had a view of the red and pink roses of a well manicured garden. We climbed the steps to get to the roof of our hotel, where we admired the view of the town. We heard echoes of conversation coming from a family of local Italians that were having lunch on a roof garden across the road. White shirts and underwear hung on the washing lines that stretched from one apartment balcony to the next, decorating the sky. For breakfast we made like the Italians and sipped an espresso while munching panettone, parmesan cheese, prosciutto, Italian salami, and local fruit. When a few restaurant owners rudely ignored our inquiries, we concluded that most Italians hate to speak English; I was glad that I had memorized some basic Italian phrases that I had learned from an Earworms audio CD before I left Cyprus.

In Rome, we walked for hours exploring romantic statues, piazzas, and fountains. The Spanish steps and the Trevi Fountain were swarmed with noisy tourists. We made the mistake of ordering a coffee and a soft drink in a busy restaurant in the famous Piazza Navona, and we were charged sixteen euros. (In Cyprus the tourists would be writing long letters of complaint to the government, but in Rome the tourists take no notice of the cost of food and drink.) After we had learned our expensive lesson, we stuck to ordering *vino rosso* [red wine] and homemade pasta in old, family-run restaurants that we found in the quieter side streets of Rome. My sister Dora still makes the best lasagne I have ever tasted. We did taste some delicious meat dishes, garlic artichokes, and simple but incredible pizza. No one makes better pizza than the Italians; their base is thin and crispy, and the toppings are few so that the tongue can taste all the flavors. For dessert we ate lemon *gelato* [ice cream] that was so good it made me forget my sorrows. My final cure was our shopping therapy, and the stylish Italian clothes and *scarpe* [shoes] that we bought. We saw a Pinocchio store that looked like a carpenter's workshop, and I could not resist buying a wooden Pinocchio souvenir. The detailed doors and door handles of the Roman buildings that we passed attracted my gaze.

In Rome there were Vespas and Minis parked on every corner. We strolled through the park of the Villa Borghese, and I pictured the ancient Romans walking the same path as we did. We explored the Castle of Saint Angelo, which was filmed in the movie Angels and Demons, and once we reached the top, we admired the view of Saint Peter's Square. In Saint Peter's Basilica I wondered how long it took for the sculptors to define the life-sized granite statues that were found everywhere. We skipped the three-hour queue around the walls of the Vatican museum because we are typical Cypriots and we paid extra to get inside more quickly with a guide. I feel obliged to tell you that the oldest sculpture inside the museum was sculpted by a Greek from Athens, whose name was inscribed on the base; this statue is said to have inspired Michaelangelo. There are no words to describe the magnificent paintings on the roof of the Sistine Chapel, which took Michaelangelo many years to complete. The Vatican must make millions every year from the tourists who visit; I wonder if that money is put to good use.

The Duomo Church in Florence has an awe-inspiring exterior and a surprisingly dull interior. After eight hours of walking from one tourist attraction to the next, I had to buy myself new sneakers. The beautiful sights of Florence were worth all the blisters on my feet. My sister shopped so much that we were forced to buy a luggage bag with wheels that we dragged with us all over Florence.

Spain

Ola from Spain in 2011! My mother and I landed at the airport in Barcelona and we were greeted by our multilingual Cypriot tour guide, Rolanthi, who explained our mission for the week and helped us settle in at our first hotel. The next few days would test Rolanthi's patience— sixty-three Cypriots with no sense of direction, half of whom lacked the ability to control their bladder, and half of whom had no control of the volume of their voice, all in one bus for six to eight hours a day, for a whole week. Absorbing all the glorious sites and historical tales of eight cities in seven days is not for the fainthearted, but I can assure you that it was worth every hour that my aching butt spent sitting on that bus seat and the annoying wake-up calls that rang in my ears at six-thirty every morning.

The Catholic cathedrals we saw in Spain are too magnificent for words, but the one that stands out in my mind is the Sagrada Familia, in Barcelona, that has been under construction for over a hundred years and that needs many more years to be completed. The fantasy of the great architect Antoni Gaudi is imprinted in all the buildings that he has designed, and one has to see them to understand the extent of his imagination. In the beautiful Park Guell, Gaudi's creative genius is expressed in some fairy-tale-like houses which are found at the entrance and in the gardens.

The first day we drove to the top of a hill called Montjuic, where we explored a Spanish village and admired the views of the city, the Olympic stadium, and the modern tower of Calatrava. On the second day we drove to Montserrat, a monastery dedicated to the Virgin Mary, which is found on a breathtaking peaked mountain top, about 1,200 meters above sea level. The third day we drove to the historical city of Gerona, where we admired the buildings that were influenced by the Jewish and Arab citizens. In the town of Figueres, we stopped at the museum of the artistic genius Salvador Dali, and we studied some of his interesting and strange art works. On the fourth day we made a stop in

Zaragoza, where we saw Catholic churches with lavish interior decor, and once again I couldn't help but wonder if the priests of those great churches played any part in feeding the poor. We then set off for the modern city of Madrid, the capital of Spain. Our first stop was the Royal palace, where the Spanish kings lived in complete luxury up until 1931. We then paid a visit to the famous Real Madrid football stadium and the bull-fighting ring.

My favorite museum in Spain was the Prado, where we admired magnificent paintings by the famous El Greco, Goya, Velazquez, and many others, and where our local tour guide told us stories about the painters' scandalous lives. In Madrid, we went out one evening to watch the passionate dance of flamenco. We followed the steps of the energetic and fiery Spanish dancers while sipping on sweet sangria and listening to the sweet melodies of a Spanish guitar.

On the sixth day we drove to the picturesque city of Toledo, which is surrounded by Gothic walls and castles and overlooks a river. We studied the home and the paintings of El Greco, and we were shown more stunning cathedrals which took hundreds of years to build. We then popped into a workshop where we were shown the art of Damascening, and we bought pendants and swords as souvenirs. We heard amusing stories about the mythical insane knight called Don Quixote, and we bought almond biscuits and treats, the specialty of that town. Our next stop was the relaxing coastal city of Valencia, which is decorated with a combination of impressive modern buildings designed by Santiago Calatrava and romantic, historical buildings of the past. In the old town I had to dodge an overweight gypsy lady who was forcing sprigs of lavender in my hands and was begging to read my fortune, in Spanish. My favorite foods in Spain were the *tapas*, which are little portions of various delicacies that sit on top of toasted bread. When we were short for time, we munched on sandwiches filled with Spanish ham and chorizo salami. We also tried the paella at two different restaurants. Paella is a dish made with rice, seafood, vegetables, chicken, and various spices such as saffron, but I was a bit disappointed because the paella I make myself is a lot tastier. At one restaurant I ate a delicious dish that appeared to be meat balls with a red sauce, but I found out at the end of the meal that they were in fact bull's testicles. For dessert we tried all the flavors of *tourron*, a Spanish sweet made with almonds and sugar, and many different flavors of the local ice cream. We quenched our thirst with a local milky drink called *Horchada*, which tasted a bit like almonds. On the last day we drove back to the airport in Barcelona, where we said *adios* to an exhausted Rolanthi, who by that stage had given up on showing the Cypriots how to stand in a single line at the check-in counter and who was probably glad to finally be free from one of her most challenging groups.

My Trip to the Other Side of the World

Australia

In 2009, thanks to technology and that wonderful invention called Facebook, I reconnected with Jennifer, my best friend from primary school. Somewhere between South Africa and Scotland, we had lost touch. We e-mailed a bit at university, but when I moved back to Cyprus, Jennifer emigrated to Australia and both our postal and e-mail addresses changed. The only reason either of us joined Facebook was to find each other. My Scottish friend came to visit me in Cyprus, and we saw each other after sixteen years of being apart. She gave me all the letters I had sent her during my school years and made me tear up with emotion. Reading those letters bought back many memories from my childhood in South Africa. I was excited to show her the island of my birth and the place I call my new home (I have written about her visit in the next chapter.)

In 2010, I flew halfway around the world to visit my friend who now lives in Brisbane, Australia. After my tiring twenty-two-hour journey, she picked me up from the airport and welcomed me into her home as if I were one of her sisters. I feel very blessed to have such great friends all over the world. The first few days I discovered the meaning of the words jet lag, because Australia is eight hours ahead of Cyprus. The jet lag, surprisingly, diminished my appetite but it did not stop our sightseeing. Jennifer is an electrical engineer, and she took leave from her work just to be my tour guide. She had a week planner on her fridge, which she had filled out with many day trips that she had planned for us. I was there for only two-and-a-half-weeks, and my thoughtful friend wanted to show me as much as possible. The first night I struggled to sleep, and I listened to the footsteps of the possums living in my friend's roof. At five o'clock the next morning, I heard squawking noises outside my bedroom window and I was surprised to see wild, red and green parrots pecking at the seeds of a bottlebrush tree in Jennifer's garden.

On my second day, we drove to the Australia Zoo, which was founded by the late Steve Irwin. I saw incredible animals, such as the sleepy koala bear, the laid-back kangaroo, the adorable wombat, the strange Tasmanian devil, the elegant cassowary bird and unusual giant lizards. The following day we drove two hours to walk on a canopy in the treetops of a real rain forest. To make our adventure more exciting, God sent rain to pour down on us. I saw some of the incredible birds of Australia, such as the lyrebird, which sings a lovely song, and the kookaburra, which preys on snakes in the bush. Just when I thought I had seen all of God's creatures, we explored a cave that had glowworms on the ceiling which gave off so much light in the dark that they shone like stars in the sky.

We walked on the white sandy beaches of the Sunshine Coast and admired the daring surfers. It was winter in Australia, and we were too cold to swim. The ibis birds were so tame that they flew inches away from our heads. At the Gold Coast, we collected shells and watched hundreds of seagulls playing tag with the waves. In the touch pools at Sea World, I touched interesting creatures, such as a slimy stingray, and I discovered that certain sharks lay eggs in strange-looking mermaid's purses. We watched an entertaining dolphin show, and if I had not been wearing my skinny jeans and boots, I would have jumped into the water to swim with those intelligent mammals.

We paid a visit to the Ginger Factory, where we ate sweet ginger treats, a nut factory, where we ate chocolate-covered macadamia nuts, and an opal gem store, where we learned about opals. Jennifer's generous mother, Liz, gave us tickets to The Nutcracker ballet at the local theater. My friend and I tried very hard to appear sophisticated and stay awake during the entire ballet. I think we preferred the movie that we saw at a gold-class movie house that was good enough for the queen.

We drove to the Tamborine Mountains and walked around the local village, exploring the stores. We saw handmade wooden cuckoo clocks, and I learned how they tell time despite their lack of electricity or batteries. We savored gourmet chocolates and different flavors of fudge. When it started to rain, we ducked into a coffee shop and ate scones with jam and sipped hot tea to warm up. One morning we went on a walking tour through the neat and organized city of Brisbane. We attended the Valentino exhibition in the Gallery of Modern Art and admired the exquisite handmade designer dresses. We admired gigantic trees, the beautiful botanical gardens of Brisbane, and the water dragons (giant lizards) that were sipping water from a pond. During my stay I ate tasty, tender beef steaks that had been cooked for many hours at an Australian restaurant called the Hog's Breath Café. I tasted some interesting fruit, such as dragon fruit and breadfruit, I ate a black bread roll that was made with bamboo, and I drank locally brewed ginger beer.

While I was in Australia, I also met up with my Muslim friend from university, Shahana, who had moved to Brisbane with her family. I spent a wonderful day with her and her three adorable children, and it was great to catch up after eight years. Shahana and her husband, Mohammed asked me to stay for dinner. They were fasting for Ramadan at the time, so they were not allowed to eat or drink anything from sunrise to sunset. We broke their fast in the evening with delicious, spicy food that my friend had prepared. Shahana told me to try the mild soup that her children were enjoying; it looked like Cypriot *trahana* soup, but when it landed on my tongue my bland taste buds caught fire and I had to swallow a bottle of water to recover. I suddenly remembered that my friend would dollop her food with the hottest Tabasco (chili) sauce when we ate out in South Africa. I did learn that chili does wonders for clearing the sinuses.

The day before I left Australia, Jennifer and I decided to go whale watching in the ocean. The captain of our ship was a pretty blond woman who played Elvis songs on the speaker radio to attract the whales. As we sailed off, we saw many dolphins in the distance. After an hour, the captain announced that it was time for lunch, and we rushed to the buffet tables inside the boat. An enormous mother whale that was the same size as our boat swam toward us with her calf, and we heard squeals of excitement from the spectators standing outside. I was annoyed that I had missed the first close encounter with the whales because I was too busy stuffing my face. I decided I had eaten enough, and I ran out to the deck as if there was no tomorrow. All of a sudden, the mother whale lifted her head out of the water and looked me straight in the eye with her small, sad-looking left eye. That moment felt holier to me than all the religious sites I have visited so far, and I felt God's presence. It is the most magnificent, graceful creature that I have ever had the privilege to see up close. Everyone should go whale watching at least once in his or her lifetime.

This may be the end of the chapter on my travels, but I hope this isn't the extent of my travels. God willing, I would like to see a new country every year until the day I die.

While I was writing my memoir, part of the city of Brisbane was flooded by torrential rains, a part of Japan was engulfed by a tsunami, certain towns in America were damaged by tornados, a honeymooner was killed by a shark in the Seychelles, foreign containers filled with explosives, exploded in a small town in Cyprus killing innocent soldiers, political protests in neighboring countries have resulted in unnecessary bloodshed.

Life is so unpredictable that we have to make the most of every single day, and we should all strive to turn our dreams into our reality.

Chapter 8:

Falling in Love
with Cyprus

L iving in Cyprus, I have learned that life is meant to be lived *yiali, ali,* [Cypriot for slowly, slowly] or *siga, siga* [Greek for slowly, slowly]. Things happen when they are meant to happen. No one is in a rush. On Wednesday afternoons, Sundays, and a few weeks in August, businesses close, and the island goes into sleep mode. In the summer, most businesses (except those in the tourist area) close between one and four o'clock in the afternoon because it gets too hot to work. Even though all the stores are air conditioned, most Cypriots would rather be at home with family, eating, napping, or drinking *frappe*. All banks close at one thirty (except for currency exchange in the tourist areas). Government offices lock their doors at midday, and they are very bureaucratic—paperwork takes months or even years to be completed. Obtaining a simple document like a title deed is challenge enough to make a property investor like Donald Trump want to change careers. A document in Cyprus is only official once it has been stamped, photocopied three times, and had every page signed by all the parties.

In our town, we throw our toilet paper in the dustbin and not in the toilet. (Thankfully, they have recently started working on a new sewerage system.) The necessary roadwork starts but never seems to end smoothly. Most Cypriots who drive double cabs believe that the parking laws do not apply to them, and you will find one in every color on every city pavement. Most Cypriot shoppers ignore yellow lines and underground parking lots because they feel the need to park as close to an entrance as possible. A few clever men have taken advantage of the lack of parking in the towns and are now turning their inherited, empty pieces of land into parking lots with tollbooths.

To survive in Cyprus, you must learn the art of patience. Eventually, you reach the conclusion that if you can't beat them, you must join them. Whether we like it or not, we did not move back to Cyprus to change the people or the country. The beauty and safety of this laid-back island make up for any inconvenience.

The time came for us to move into our own place. With the help of a good lawyer and an "ugly" mortgage, we bought a small house in a quiet mountain village in Paphos. The first thing you learn when you buy a home in Cyprus is that you need fly screens on all the windows—unless you don't mind getting bitten by mosquitoes and sharing your home with an adorable pink lizard called the misharo. Before we learned this valuable lesson, I came home to find a brown, hairy tarantula the size of my hand climbing up the staircase, apparently heading for the bedroom. I instinctively called out to my tall, "strong" husband to save the day; Nick's eyes popped out of his head when he saw the size of the spider. He ran outside and came back with our four-meter-long pool brush. His master plan was to entice the spider to climb onto the end of the pool brush, and then he would release it outside. The spider ignored the brush and hopped back down the stairs and into a vase. (Never assume that your husband is smarter than a spider.) After exterminating the spider, I called the fly screen man to come measure our windows.

When you live on a holiday island, besides the visiting spiders, you are also guaranteed annual human visitors. It is a pleasure for me to have family and friends visit my birthplace because I get to practice my tour guiding skills. A few years ago, my dear Israeli friend Rina and my sweet sister-in-law, Nadya, came for a short visit. My husband drove us three hours away to visit the fishing village of Ayia Napa. We played beach tennis on beaches with white sand and we swam in turquoise waters. At the sea caves of Cavo Greco, we watched my daring husband dive off a ridiculously high cliff into the clear waters below. We drove past huge rolls of wheat stacked up in the dry fields on our way to the town square, where we explored a monastery that was built in the fifteenth century. At a nearby tavern, we ordered meze—small plates of various tasty Cypriot snacks that keep coming until one is popping. We danced all night with the tourists in various elaborate theme pubs found on the long cobbled streets of Ayia Napa. That night we discovered why Ayia Napa has been compared to Ibiza.

In Paphos we went for a drive with my sister-in-law to see the Adonis Falls, a small waterfall hidden away in a valley. As we passed an old lady feeding her anorexic donkey, we were greeted by a giant statue of the Greek god Adonis (one of the lovers of the goddess Aphrodite). The humorous and hospitable Mr. Pambos, the owner of the land, implored us to touch the "jewels" (private part) of the statue in order to become more fertile and have a lot of children—Mr. Pambos I am still waiting for the miracle to happen!

The wonderful thing about living in Cyprus is that no matter where you live on the island, you are not too far away from the enticing waters of the Mediterranean Sea. Our waters are safe for swimming as we have calm waves, no sharks, and no deadly jellyfish. I love snorkeling with my husband, and I will never forget my first encounter with a turtle. One Sunday afternoon, we were swimming in the Akamas, the northwest peninsula of Cyprus. It is a nature reserve area, untouched by developers, and a popular egg-laying area for turtles. As I swam at leisure, admiring a scarlet-red starfish, I noticed a shadow on the sandy floor. When I looked up, I came face to face with a large green turtle that was scrutinizing me with its beady eyes. At that moment, I wondered if turtles were vegetarians. After a few minutes, I became frightened, and I screeched out loud under the water to get my husband's attention. The startled turtle pulled its head back into its shell, turned onto its stomach, and swam away as fast as it could. Whoever said turtles are slow has obviously never swum after one!

My husband then discovered a few spiky sea urchins on the sea floor and I made him fish them out. We bashed one open with a stone, and naturally I had to taste the filling, as I had seen that done on a travel show; it was disappointing, it tasted like fishy sea sludge. We decided to dry off and worship the sun. We were all alone on a long stretch of beach with our very own private lagoon. After a while, a four-by-four, double cab drove up to the shore and parked on the sand nearby. A middle-aged Cypriot man with a long black moustache got out of the car, took off all his clothes, and jumped into the sea without a care in the world. We found it amusing and tried very hard not to stare. After a while he stepped out of the water, put his underpants back on, grabbed something out of the back of his double cab, and started walking toward us. As he got closer, we saw that he held a small watermelon in his hands, which he generously offered us, perhaps as a peace offering for showing us his "jewels" or perhaps, as my husband suggests, he just wanted a close up view of my bikini. We were thirsty so we gladly accepted, and the kind stranger cut it up for us with his pocketknife. It was one of the sweetest watermelons I have ever tasted.

One winter's day, we decided to revisit the Akamas and go on a hiking trip with my five-year-old godchild, Savvaki, through the Avakas Gorge. Our hiking buddies were, my husband's friend John (who is a chef), his wife, Nadia (who is a teacher), and their son, Leon, who is the same age as Savvaki. We wore our Wellingtons because we knew that we would have to cross shallow streams since it was just after the rainy season. As we passed ancient-looking trees that stood on green pastures, we heard the buzzing sound of the bumblebees that were sitting on the purple thorn flowers, and we spotted a family of wild guinea fowl scuffling about on a cliff top. We crossed unusual rock formations while we followed the stream through a narrow pathway that is surrounded by mighty rocks on either side. The moss-covered rocks on opposing sides leaned closer to each other as we entered the gorge. As we walked deeper inside the gorge I was splashed by water droplets that dripped down from a few stalactites above my head. We eventually reached a small waterfall, but we had to turn back because the water had reached our knees. The kids enjoyed getting wet in the stream, and they picked up tiny rocks and sticks along the way.

On the way out of the Akamas, there are two isolated restaurants that run on a generator. One of these restaurants owns a few farm animals, and we usually make a stop to observe the animals. We have seen goats and sheep crossing the road with their lambs, pigs playing in the mud, and on another occasion we watched as two horses embraced while their foal stood patiently nearby. I hope that the Akamas will remain a protected nature reserve and that the tourists and locals who visit will respect the area by not littering, so that we can save it for future generations.

Cyprus is virtually crime free, and women feel safe to walk alone wherever they like. (Occasionally there are a few robberies, but the thieves are usually caught because hiding spots are rare on an island.) The scenic town of Paphos is a great place for taking long walks. I love to walk along the sea, behind the hotels, by the old lighthouse, or along the nature trails of the hills and mountains. The spectacular wild flowers come to life in the spring, after the winter rains. During my walks, I have seen different colored orchids, red poppies, pink anemones, yellow daisies, cyclamen, hyacinths, narcissus, rockrose, wild garlic flowers, chamomile flowers, wild purple lavender, and many more whose names I do not know. When I study the exquisite color and symmetry of various flowers, I can't understand how anyone can deny God's existence.

Green Monday is the first day of the long fast before Easter, and every year, when the weather permits, we celebrate this day by going into the fields and enjoying picnics with our relatives. The fields are lush and green that time of the year. We eat various green salads, vegetables, lentil dips, unleavened and fasting bread, and charcoal-grilled octopus or squid. (A few of our sneaky orthodox ancestors decided that creatures like octopus and squid are not meat and have no blood, and can therefore be eaten during the long fast.) My young cousins attempt to fly their kites, since it is very windy that time of the year. While I was taking a walk through a field in the hills of Steni village, I found many peculiar and fragile marine fossils and large oyster shells sticking out of a cliff edge—evidence that once upon a time my mother's village was under the sea.

One sunny afternoon, while my husband and I were walking our dog in our neighborhood, Nick suddenly stopped in his tracks and bellowed, "Stop! You stood on a snake!" Startled, I turned around and saw a brown-spotted snake with a squashed head and a bright red tongue sticking out the side of its mouth. The snake's body was still swooping from side to side. I later found out that it was one of the venomous snakes of Cyprus. I was very lucky that I had stood on the snake's head and not its tail. I was ten kilos heavier back then and was never more relieved to be overweight. My overindulgence on village bread and my grandmother's prayers and blessings must have saved me that day!

Being a working adult is great because you get to buy the toys you did not have as a child. I decided to buy myself a bicycle. It took me a while to regain my balance, but I eventually learned to ride in a straight line. One Saturday morning, I decided to take a ride around my block. The streets near my house are very steep, and since I was speeding down the hill, I pressed the breaks to slow down. Before I knew what was happening, the bicycle stopped moving, the back tire lifted up, and it threw me off like a wild horse. I managed to get up, ignore the loud banging noise in my head, and push my evil bicycle back up the road to my home. After a while I realized my hands couldn't reach my face. I managed to send a message for help and I was rushed to the doctor. I had fractured both my elbows—only I could get that right! I saw it as my punishment from God because a few days before, I had been complaining that I was overworked and needed a break. The second lesson I learned from that experience is that I was not born to be a sports champion, and my father had good reason not to buy me a bicycle when I was young. For two weeks, I was engulfed in humiliation as my mother (my designated nurse) had to wipe my butt, bathe me, and feed me like an infant. After a month, thanks to the amazing healing powers of the human body, I was back to normal. I now thank God for the ability to use my hands. If a tree heals up after its branches are broken off, than we should not expect any less of our bones.

One rainy Sunday, as we were driving out of Steni village, the sun decided to peep over the rain clouds. I reminded my husband to look out for rainbows. God granted me my wish because when I looked behind me I spotted a magnificent double rainbow in the horizon. We immediately drove to the top of the hill to immortalize the scene with our camera. I believe rainbows are miracles and a reminder from God that better days will come, no matter what obstacles we face on this earth.

Winters in Cyprus are very mild; we only get three months a year of really cold weather, when it snows up in the mountains. The first time I saw snow was in Cyprus. (While we lived in Johannesburg, South Africa, it never snowed—our Christmas days were always sunny.) During our first February in Cyprus, my brother-in-law Sotiris drove us to the Troodos Mountains in his jeep. It was a two-hour windy drive to the top. As we entered the peak of the mountain, my excitement grew when I saw white blobs on the side of the road. Once we got to Mount Olympus, the highest point, the snow was about two meters high. We bounced out of the car, and it felt like we had stepped into a fridge. We forgot our age and had snowball fights like carefree children. I built my first snowman, and we sat on flat plastic spades and sledded down the snowy slopes. We explored the local village square and were offered roasted, sugarcoated nuts by the stall vendors. We ate *souvlakia* (small pork kebabs served with salad and lemon in Cypriot pita bread), which warmed up our cold fingers. We bought red toffee apples and locally made *shoushouko*, which is the specialty of the town. We covered the bonnet of the car with snow, hoping to take it back home. Cyprus is one of the few places in the world where, in the same day, you can walk along the sea and play in the snow in the highest mountains.

During another excursion to the mountains, my husband and I explored the village of Kakopetria. Our hotel was composed of old, stone houses that had been converted into hotel rooms. As we walked through the cobbled streets on our way to our room, I felt as though I was walking back in time. Our room had a stone fireplace and a traditional four-poster bed. We heard the trickling noise of a stream outside our window. The stream is formed by the clean mountain water that comes from the higher peaks of Troodos, and it leads to a small waterfall. On our way back home, we made a stop in the village of Omodhos, which is famous for its vineyards and we lit a candle in the Byzantine church of the Monastery of Stavros, surrounded by the scent of burning wax and sweet-smelling incense.

My favorite mountain village is called Lefkara, which is found in the province of Larnaca. It is famous for its lace and cut-out, embroidered linen, and it has many traditional village homes which were built with white stones. The architecture of many of the buildings has been influenced by the Venetians that once ruled Cyprus. During our visit I bought a few pieces of delicate lace, and I watched an old lady with deft fingers embroider a linen table cloth. We were told that Leonardo da Vinci was inspired by the patterns on the linen from Lefkara during his visit to Cyprus. The patience that is needed for such elaborate needle work is unfortunately missing from our generation. My mother insists that Facebook and computers will be the death of handmade lace; I am afraid she may be right.

I grew up in a village and later in a quiet suburb, so I am not a very big fan of the city. One weekend, I decided to be more daring and drive to the busy city of Nicosia to visit Dina, my mother's first cousin. Nicosia (also called Lefkosia) is the capital of Cyprus. Dina's family is loving, kind, and very hospitable. Dina and her father *theo* Dyonisios, who is my maternal grandfather's brother, are passionate historians, and they were excellent tour guides. As we walked through the old city of Nicosia, admiring the architecture of the restored houses, Dina told us the history of the Lusignans (from France) and the Venetians that ruled Cyprus over five hundred years ago. I was fascinated by the story of Caterina Cornaro, the last Venetian queen of Cyprus. The Venetians have left behind impressive city walls which decorate the city. It is interesting to learn about all the different nations that have ruled and fought over this little island. Beautiful, old churches and mosques are scattered throughout the city. Sadly, Nicosia has been divided by the Green line since 1974. The Green line separates the Greek and Turkish parts of the island, and it runs through the middle of the city. With a heavy heart, *theo* Dyonisio showed us his abandoned house near the Green line, which he was forced to evacuate during the devastating war.

As I mentioned in the previous chapter, in August of 2009, my friend Jennifer came to visit me in Cyprus. She was intrigued by my country's nine-thousand-year-old history because she lives in a city that is only two hundred years old. Many nations have stepped on Cyprus over the years, and they have all left something behind for us to discover. I found a friend that loves archeology as much as I do, and we visited most of the ruins and museums on the island. Cyprus is an archeologist's dream. The builders in Paphos often encounter ancient pottery (and occasionally whole towns) during their excavations, and they have to stop digging. (Most of the time they probably keep quiet because it is less profitable to give up the land to the government.) Many farmers have found pottery in their fields while planting their crops. Ancient shipwrecks have also been discovered in our waters, some dating to thousands of years before the birth of Christ. Inside a few of the pots from the wrecks, they have found olive stones and remnants of red wine, which tells me that our diet in Cyprus is not that different from our ancestors. Jennifer and I walked for hours exploring the three-thousand- year-old mosaics of Kato Paphos, which is a World Heritage site. The mosaic floors depict scenes from the everyday life of the ancient Greeks and the gods that they worshipped. The mosaic tiles were put together using different-colored sea pebbles, and their color has been preserved throughout all these years. We studied the ruins of the town where the ancient Greeks lived and the amphitheater where they gathered for entertainment. We explored many caves in Paphos that have probably been around since the age of the caveman and might have been occupied by lepers during the time of Christ. We visited the museum of the Mycenaean colonization of Cyprus in Coral Bay, where copper tools were found that date from the late Bronze Age. Cyprus is named after the ancient word for copper because the mineral was mined in the past and exported by ship to the neighboring countries. In Paphos we also explored the Tombs of the Kings, where wealthy ancient Greeks were buried.

In the province of Limassol we explored the ruins of Kourion. We walked through ancient villas with mosaic floors that once belonged to some wealthy Romans. We sat on the top steps of the ancient amphitheater to admire the glorious sea view; occasionally one can spot paragliders in the distance. At the Sanctuary of Apollo, we touched the ancient stone columns, and at Kolossi Castle, where the knights of St. John once lived, we climbed the winding steps to get to the top. We passed an old sugar refinery on the way out.

On the way back home, we made a stop in the village of Kouklia to visit the Sanctuary of Aphrodite. There were many ancient exhibits in the museum, including a large stone that represented Aphrodite and was worshipped by pilgrims. Our next stop was the village of Lemba and its ancient Neolithic archeological site. In this area, archeologists have found statues of the fertility goddess amongst other pottery. They have recreated a few houses, according to the design of the circular stone foundations that were found on the site. The houses are constructed of mud and straw, and they remind me of some of the primitive African huts that I saw in South Africa. In Paphos we explored the ruins at Saint Paul's pillar, where, according to the Bible, the Apostle Paul was flogged before converting the Roman governor of that time to Christianity.

Not far from Saint Paul's pillar, one can find the catacomb of Ayia Solomoni, where our Christian ancestors used to hide from the Romans and Ottoman Turks, to practice their religion. There is a tired-looking tree above the catacomb that is brimming with handkerchiefs and pieces of cloth that were tied by the faithful as they prayed to the saint for a cure for their sick loved ones. In the village square of Yeroskipou, there is a dome-shaped, Byzantine church called Ayia Paraskevi, and we lit a candle in front of the sad eyes of the Virgin Mary. Across the road from the church there are a few stores that sell hand-woven baskets and various flavors of sweet *loukoumia*, which are Cypriot delights—also known as Turkish delights, depending on who made them.

Jennifer bought souvenirs from the *agora* [market] in Paphos town, and we ate *baklava* at the tiny restaurant by the Turkish hammam [baths]. We walked along the sea path, behind the hotels in Kato Paphos until we reached the old castle at the harbor. We sat in one of the modern coffee shops and drank a refreshing *frapechino* [sweet, milky coffee with crushed ice] and a freshly squeezed orange juice that was made with locally grown oranges.

Jennifer loved the grilled *halloumi* cheese that we ate at the traditional taverns, and she was stunned when she saw that the fish was served with the head on and the bones in the middle. I ordered some sweet red wine called *coumandaria*, which was originally made for the English kings that ruled Cyprus in the past. Back at my house, I prepared Greek coffee and read my friend's fortune from her cup—just for laughs—like my aunt Maria used to do with us.

In the town of Polis, where time has stood still for the last thirty years, we ate my favorite homemade ice cream at the run-down coffee shop near the square. I can be a real pain in the butt when it comes to enforcing Cypriot food on friends' taste buds. I made Jennifer try some local flavors like *triantafilo* [rose] and *masticha* [a resin with a distinct flavor that is difficult to describe, it comes from the bark of a tree. It is used often in Greek cake recipes, it is made into various products including gum, and it is also helpful in treating stomach ulcers]. I have asked the elderly ice-cream man for his recipe many times before, but he always tells me that it is a family secret.

One Saturday morning, we picked up my sister Dora and my five-year-old godchild, Savvaki, and we went swimming in the tranquil, clear waters of Latchi. My friend collected a few of the tiny multicolored pebbles from the beach, and after we failed to teach Savvaki how to swim, we buried him in the pebbles instead. Later that afternoon we explored the Baths of Aphrodite, a cove where the ancient Greek goddess of love is said to have bathed.

Village Bread, Olive Oil and a Grandmother's Blessings

The following day we drove to the famous tourist site called Petra tou Romiou, which is a little bay protected by two big rocks. It is said to be the birthplace of the Greek goddess Aphrodite, who rose from the waves. (Cyprus is also known as the Island of Aphrodite.) The smaller of the two rocks was supposedly thrown into the sea by a Greek with superhuman strength who was trying to sink the ships of Arab raiders. According to another myth, one of Aphrodite's jealous lovers tossed the rock into the sea while in a fit of rage. Inspired by the love stories of Aphrodite, many lovebirds have left behind pebbled hearts enclosing their initials in the sand and hill surrounding the rocks.

Early one morning my uncle Theo took us on a scenic, two-hour drive to visit Kykkos, the wealthiest monastery in Cyprus. The mountains on route are composed of a thick, dense forest, and the clean, crisp air is filled with the scent of pine. The nuns are very strict with the dress code, and we had to cover our exposed legs with purple robes that they provided. The monastery is adorned with golden mosaics and icons made with real gold. It is home to a famous icon of the Virgin Mary, which is said to have been painted by St. Luke the Evangelist while the Virgin was still alive. Invaders burned the monastery several times in the past, but the icon has miraculously survived. The new museum of the monastery has an impressive collection of Christian Byzantine paintings and religious relics.

We paid our respects at the nearby tomb of Archbishop Makarios. On the way down, we stopped to see the nature reserve at Stavros tis Psokas, which protects the mouflon, the wild mountain goats of Cyprus. My gift to Jennifer was a personal tour of the villages where I grew up, and I introduced her to some of my relatives. We stopped to observe the farming and cooking tools that my great-grandparents used in their daily lives, at the new museum in Steni village that was built by the *mouhtari* Elias, the efficient mayor of the village. I showed my friend what a carob tree looks like, and I made her taste *anari* cheese drizzled with sweet carob syrup. That evening we went to the festival of the grape in Lysso village, where we ate traditional wedding food and watched Cypriot folk dancing. On the Sunday before she left, my father made his famous lamb *souvla*, and my mother made her specialty, *koubebia*, which is grape leaves stuffed with a mixture of rice and minced pork meat (that is fried with finely chopped onions, mint, and grated tomatoes) and served with fresh lemon juice. For dessert we ate *mahalepi*, which is a refreshing jellylike pudding, made with corn flour, sugar, and water and served cold with water and sweet rose syrup.

I love to walk through my father's meticulously kept orchard in Steni. This is where my father spends all his free time, taking care of his pampered older "children"—his citrus and olive trees. My father plucks the weeds around their trunks with such determination that one would think his own feet are the roots in the soil fighting for space and nutrients.

Once a year, when the olives are ready, my parents and relatives spend many long hours picking them off the trees. Once their boxes are full, they take them to the local olive mill and make their own virgin olive oil. When the olive oil is ready, my father gives all the relatives a big bottle. Olive oil is used in most Cypriot recipes, and it is as important as water in Cyprus. I have read many articles on how the Mediterranean diet is one of the healthiest in the world, and scientists have shown that olive oil is one of the secrets.

When the walnuts and almonds are edible, my mother sits for hours breaking the shells open and filling plastic bags with the nutmeats, which she shares amongst us. When the oranges, mandarins, grapefruit, sweet lemons, bergamots, and lemons are ripe, my father shares the fruit with the whole family. I always believed that if I planted an orange pip (seed) in the ground, it would grow into a tree and make sweet oranges. When I asked my father, he laughed and told me that I would eat bitter oranges. He then explained the process of propagation or how a wild orange tree is fooled into growing edible oranges. My father may have not attended high school, but when it comes to his knowledge of trees, he deserves a degree.

My father has converted the container that he brought from South Africa, into a kind of greenhouse. He has painted the exterior green, and he has planted grape vines all around it; they have grown tall and entwined, providing shade during the hot summers.

The gods of Olympus would be impressed by the ripe bunches of red grapes that hang off the vines in September. It has become a picnic site for our family.

Around his container, my father grows avocados, beans, cucumbers, tomatoes, lettuce, onions, peppers, cauliflower, watermelon, sweet melons, pumpkins, zucchinis, eggplants, papaya trees, cactus fruit trees, apricots, plums, guava fruit trees, and more. My mother's simple kitchen in Paphos usually looks like a cluttered fruit and vegetable market. My parents hate to throw food away, so ripe tomatoes are turned into tomato paste, surplus vegetables are frozen or pickled, ripe fruit is made into jam, surplus lemons are turned into lemonade, citrus peels are turned into Cypriot sweets, and stale bread is turned into breadcrumbs. On my mother's washing line in her backyard, competing for space with the wet clothing, one can usually find bunches of wild oregano, thyme, mint, or my father's *loukanika* and *lountza* (Cypriot sausages and ham) hanging out to dry.

My sisters and I are very fortunate that we have a father with green thumbs. He has planted all our gardens, and he regularly visits to maintain his art work. He refuses to take money from any of us for all his gardening work because he says it is his duty as a father. We have tried to take him out for dinner many times but he tells us he would rather buy lamb and make *souvla*.

My father spends more time with his grandchildren than he ever did with us, and he shows them a lot of love. My sister's house is built on my father's orchard, and so her children see their grandfather often. Savvaki, wants to be just like his *pappou*. On the weekends, Savvaki puts on his miniature army outfit and boots and runs off into the orchard to help his *pappou* with the trees. He loves to prune trees and pick olives with his grandfather. Savvaki and his younger brother sit on their toy tractor and follow my father around the orchard for hours. Hopefully, my father's grandchildren will learn his agricultural tricks and take care of his trees when they are older.

Thanks to Woud, a patient who is a hot-air balloon pilot, Nick and I had the privilege of enjoying a hot-air balloon ride over Paphos. (Unfortunately the hot-air balloon was banned in Cyprus, shortly thereafter.) Woud, who is from Holland, called me at five o'clock one morning to tell me that he had two seats open in his basket, and he asked if I was interested. I instantly said yes, hopped out of bed, and dragged my sleepy husband with me. Once we were at the take off location, my husband helped the men hold up the enormous balloon that was stretched out across a field, while it was being filled with the hot air from the fire. Once it was upright, eight of us hopped into the basket. The hot-air balloon lifted up very slowly and peacefully, just like a feather. Guided by our pilot and the wind, the balloon ascended until we were higher than the clouds.

We admired the deep blue sea, the shimmering dams, the green plantations on the hillsides, and the pine-tree covered mountains in the distance. We watched as the bright sun rose above the sea and stretched out its arms on the horizon. I leaned over the side, thousands of feet from the ground, and I was inspired to pray. First I prayed for the hot-air balloon to stay safely in the air until we landed, and then I thanked God for my family, and for all of my blessings. The people below looked like tiny ants. At times, we get so caught up in the petty problems of our daily lives that we lose sight of what we really are in the greater scope of the universe. In reality, we are nothing but hungry little ants that crawl around on a beautifully painted rock that rose up from the sea a very long time ago.

When God decides it is my time, I will be buried in the soil, alongside the bones of my grandmothers, with some village bread and some olive oil. So in the meantime, I vow to live this life to the full and eat a lot of glorious food on the way.

Life is what we make of it. We either focus on the wall
or search for the sun in the distance!

Chapter 9:

A Few of my Favorite Family recipes

These recipes have been passed on to me from family members and friends, so the measurements might not be consistent. Measurements may be converted to the units of your choice using an online calculator.

Many of these foods have been mentioned in previous chapters in this book.

Kalin Orexi! (Bon Appetit)

Starters
Dad's Wild Mushrooms
(Serves 4)

Ingredients:

•4 large, fresh, edible red mushrooms (from the forest or supermarket)

•Juice of 1 lemon
•Olive oil
•Salt for taste

Method:

Grill mushrooms in a fan oven or cook on a grill over a fireplace 15-20 minutes or until the mushrooms are crispy on the edges, depending on your preference. Serve with a drizzle of lemon juice and olive oil, and sprinkle with salt. You can also fry the mushrooms in a pan for 10 minutes, with a little olive oil and 2 cloves of crushed garlic; serve with lemon juice and salt.

Mom's Cypriot-Style Snails
(Serves 6)

Ingredients:

• Pick snails from a clean garden or hillside where there is no litter, pesticide, or doggie poop. Pick enough snails to fill about half a bucket. Snails usually come out just after the rain, so that's a good time to hunt for them, or you can buy them ready from a snail farm.

•$^1/_2$ cup olive oil
•$^1/_2$ cup red wine vinegar
•Few sprigs of fresh parsley
•Salt for taste

Method:

Place snails in a bucket with a perforated lid and feed them flour, or lettuce and rosemary sprigs for three days to clean out their intestines (and give them a better taste). Wash the snails well and boil

them in a pot until all the slime rises to the surface, drain water and repeat process until all the slime and mucus is gone. Drain water and serve with a dipping sauce of olive oil, red wine vinegar, finely chopped parsley, and salt. Use a toothpick to get the snail out of its shell, and, using your fingers, pull off the mucky end bit that is not eaten. Dip the edible bit in the sauce. Snails can also be served with a lemon-butter-garlic sauce.

Mom's Green Olives

Ingredients:

- Fresh green olives (preferably just picked off the tree)
- Plenty of fresh water
- Fresh lemon juice
- 1 cup salt
- Grape vine leaves or bay leaves
- Olive oil
- Oregano (preferably wild)
- 2-3 cloves garlic, whole or crushed
- Bread for dipping

Method:

Break the olives open with a stone or hammer on a flat surface, place them into a glass storage jar, cover with water, add freshly squeezed lemon juice to preserve their color, and place lid on top. Change and drain water daily for 4 days, adding ¼ cup lemon juice each time. On the 5th day, dissolve 1 cup salt to 5 cups water and add this to the jar. Add freshly squeezed lemon juice, cover olives with grape vine leaves or a few bay leaves, and close jar. Allow to set for 3 months. When you would like to eat some olives, take a few out of the jar, rinse well, place in a bowl, and add lemon juice, olive oil, oregano, and chopped garlic, or whole garlic if you do not want to eat the garlic. Eat the olives and dip some bread in the tasty dressing.

Tarama Dip

Ingredients:

- 125 grams tarama (fish roe that is sold in a jar in Greek supermarkets)
- 3 medium potatoes (boiled, mashed, and cooled)
- Juice of 2 lemons
- 1 small grated onion
- Pita bread

Method:

Blend all ingredients together (except the pita bread) in a food processor until smooth and serve in a bowl as a dip with warm pita bread.

Tzatziki or Talatouri Dip

Ingredients:

- 1 small cucumber, grated
- 500 milliliters thick plain yogurt
- 2 teaspoons dry mint
- 2 crushed garlic cloves
- Juice of half a lemon
- Salt for taste
- Pita bread

Method:

After grating cucumber, drain liquid and mix together with the rest of the ingredients (except the pita bread) until smooth. Serve as a dip with toasted garlic bread or warm pita bread.

Fried Halloumi

Method:

Slice Halloumi cheese into thick slices, dip in flour, and fry in olive oil until golden on both sides. Serve with a squeeze of lemon juice.

Breads-Muffins-Res

Granny Theodora's Village Bread

Ingredients:

•1 packet instant yeast (my granny used to make her own, but it is too complicated to explain)
•1 teaspoon sugar
•$^1/_2$ cup warm water

•4 cups white bread flour
•1 teaspoon salt
•$^1/_4$ cup olive oil
•Sesame seeds, aniseed, and cumin for the top

Method:

Mix yeast, sugar, and water together in a bowl and leave for 10 minutes. Add flour, salt, and olive oil, and knead until the dough is soft and not sticky (if sticky, add a bit more flour). Leave the dough in the bowl covered with a wet cloth and allow to rise for 2 to 3 hours. Shape dough into a ball or oval and sprinkle with sesame seeds, aniseed, and cumin. Place on wax paper on a tray and bake for 40 minutes or until golden brown in a preheated oven at 180 degrees Celsius.

Olive Bread

Method:

Olive Bread: Make as above but add $1^1/_2$ cups stoned, chopped brown olives, 1 teaspoon dry mint, 1 teaspoon black pepper, 2 teaspoons chopped parsley, and 1 finely chopped onion to the dough.

Mom's Cypriot Halloumi Bread

Ingredients:

- 1 cup olive oil
- 5 eggs
- 250 grams halloumi cheese, grated
- Pinch of fresh mint

- 3 cups white bread flour
- 3 teaspoons baking powder
- Pinch of mastic powder
- Sesame seeds for the top
- 1 cup water

Method:

Beat the oil and eggs together. Add halloumi, mint, and all dry ingredients, then water. Knead to make dough; if dough is sticky, add a bit of flour. Shape dough into a long oval shape and sprinkle outer areas with sesame seeds. Slice indentations on top with a knife for decoration and ease of cutting slices once ready. Bake at 160 degrees Celsius for 50 minutes

Mom's Flaounes (Cypriot Easter bread rolls/tarts)
(Makes 30 flaounes)
(Warning: Eating too many may lead to constipation!)

Ingredients:

Dough:
- 6 cups bread flour
- 25 grams fresh yeast
- 1 cup warm water
- 1 cup warm milk
- 1 teaspoon salt
- 2 tablespoons sugar
- 1 teaspoon mastic powder
- 1 teaspoon cinnamon
- $^1/_2$ cup melted butter
- Sesame seeds, egg for glazing
- 2 teaspoons dried mint
- 250 grams raisins (optional)

Filling:
- 450 grams halloumi cheese
- 250 grams cheddar cheese
- 125 grams pecorino cheese
- 2 tablespoon semolina
- 1 teaspoon baking powder
- 4 beaten eggs

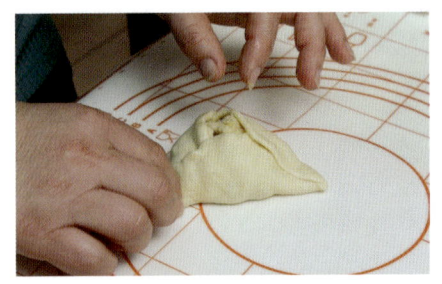

Method:

The cheese must be hard; therefore, purchase a week before preparation and store uncovered in the fridge.

Coarsely grate the cheese into a bowl and leave loosely covered with a cloth overnight. The next morning make the dough:

Dissolve yeast in $^1/_4$ cup warm water. Stir in sugar, remaining $^3/_4$ cup water, and milk, mix, and leave aside. Sift 5 cups of flour, salt, mastic powder, and cinnamon in a bowl; stir in melted butter and then yeast mixture. Stir with a wooden spoon till dough comes away from the sides of the bowl. If too sticky, add more flour. Place dough on a floured board and knead well until smooth, adding flour as required. Place dough in a lightly oiled bowl, turn, and coat with oil. Cover and leave to rise in a warm place for 2 hours. While dough is rising, make the filling. Add all the ingredients to the cheese and stir well until it forms a stiff paste. Shape dough into 30 balls and place on a floured board; keep covered. Roll each ball into a 10-centimeter circle (not too thin). Place a good tablespoon of filling in the middle of the circle and fold in the dough at 3 points to make a triangle, making sure that the filling is well enclosed with a small opening at the center of each flaouna. Brush flaouna with beaten egg and sprinkle with sesame seed. Place on greased baking tray and leave to rest for 45 minutes. Bake at 220 degrees Celsius for about 20 minutes. Serve warm or cold.

Mom's Healthy Muffins

(Makes about 24 small muffins)

Ingredients:

- 3 eggs
- 1 cup brown sugar
- $1/_2$ cup sunflower oil
- 500 milliliters milk
- Vanilla essence
- $2^1/_2$ cups whole wheat flour
- $2^1/_2$ teaspoons bicarbonate of soda
- $1/_2$ teaspoon salt
- 500 milliliters all-bran flakes
- $1/_2$ cup raisins
- Cinnamon

Method:

Beat eggs well with mixer, mix in the sugar, and add all liquid ingredients and then all the dry ingredients. Put in fridge overnight. Next morning stir and pour spoon fulls in to greased muffin trays. Cook for 25 minutes at 160 degree Celsius.

Mom's Spanakopita (Spinach Pie)

Ingredients:

- 4 spring onions and 2 medium onions, finely chopped
- 4 tablespoons olive oil
- 1$^1/_2$ kilograms fresh spinach, washed and chopped
- 500 grams feta cheese, crumbled
- 2 eggs, beaten
- 1 tablespoon chopped dill
- Salt, pepper
- 2 ready, thick pastry dough sheets
- Pinch of sesame seeds.

Method:

Fry onions in a little olive oil until soft, add spinach, and cook over very low heat until water has evaporated. Cool and add rest of ingredients except for pastry dough sheets; mix well. On the bottom of a buttered, medium sized Pyrex dish, place 1 pastry sheet after it has been brushed gently with olive oil. Fill with the filling, cover with the other sheet of pastry dough, gently brush top layer with liquid butter or olive oil, and tuck in at the sides. Pierce the top randomly with a fork and sprinkle with sesame seeds. Bake at 180 degrees Celsius for about 1 hour or until pastry is crispy and golden brown.

Soups
(These soups serve a family of 5)

My Chicken Soup

This is my version of avgolemoni, the traditional egg-lemon soup. It's delicious and very nutritious; it helps when you are feeling ill or sad.

Ingredients:

•Plenty of fresh water
•1 whole raw chicken, washed, with the insides removed (or a few raw chicken pieces)
•3 whole carrots, washed and peeled
•3 celery sticks
•Salt and pepper to taste

•1 cup basmati rice (if you prefer the soup thick, add more)
•A small plate of finely chopped carrot, celery, and parsley
•2 eggs
•Juice of 4 lemons (if you do not like lemon, use 2)

Method:

Put the chicken in a deep pot and cover completely with water. Bring to a boil and then lower the heat. Once the chicken starts to boil, brown froth will rise to the surface, and this must be skimmed off. After half an hour add a few whole carrots, celery sticks, and a pinch of salt and pepper. It takes at least an hour for the chicken to be ready; check with a fork, and if the meat comes away easily with the fork and it is a white color, then the chicken is ready. Remove the chicken and vegetables and place in separate bowl. Top up the pot of chicken stock with more water and add more salt and pepper to taste. Add the rice, chopped vegetables and parsley, and simmer for another 15 minutes. Once the rice is soft, turn off the heat, move the pot away from the hot plate of the stove, and add 1 cup of cold water to the pot.

For the egg-lemon sauce: In a bowl, using an electric mixer, mix the eggs with the lemon juice until a thick froth starts to form. To this froth, add a big spoonful or cup of the hot chicken stock from the pot, mixing continuously on slow speed. Add another 2 or 3 cups of chicken stock to the bowl, mixing continuously on low speed, so that the egg does not curdle. Then pour the mixed egg-lemon sauce into the pot of chicken stock, stirring continuously. The soup is ready; add a few small pieces of the cooked chicken breast to your soup and enjoy! The chicken and whole vegetables can also be eaten separately, with some lemon and salt.

Trahana Soup

Method:

Buy a packet of trahana from a Greek supermarket or from the lady in the village who makes it. You can also use 2 liters of plain chicken stock to make Trahana Soup. Soak 2 cups of trahana in 2 cups of boiling water for half an hour. Simply add the soaked trahana pieces to the chicken stock, bring to a boil, and then simmer on low heat for 30 minutes. Add some cubes of halloumi to the soup, and pepper, salt, and lemon to taste.

Mom's Chickpea Soup

Ingredients:

- 500 grams dried chickpeas
- Water
- 2 onions, finely chopped
- $1/_2$ cup olive oil
- Salt, pepper, and lemon juice

Method:

Soak chickpeas in warm water overnight. Drain and put peas in a pot of cold water; boil for 10 minutes. Drain and discard water. Add enough cold water to cover peas and bring to the boil, skimming off the foaming residue. Add onions, cover, and simmer for 2-3 hours until tender, adding more water if necessary. Add oil, salt, and pepper to taste. Simmer a few minutes and serve with lemon juice.

My version of Prawn-Thai Soup

Ingredients:

- 2 chopped spring onions
- Sunflower oil
- 2 cloves garlic
- 1 chili pepper, chopped, with only a few seeds
- 500 grams deveined prawns, without the heads and shells
- A piece of fresh, peeled ginger root
- Plenty of fresh water
- $1/_2$ cup soy sauce
- $1/_4$ cups sweet chili sauce
- A handful of rice noodles
- 2 lettuce leaves sliced
- 2 cabbage leaves finely sliced
- Fresh Lemon juice

Method:

In a nonstick wok or deep frying pan, fry the spring onions in a bit of sunflower oil over medium heat until soft. Add the cloves of garlic and remove and discard when golden. Add chili. Add prawns and stir. Add ginger root for fragrance, it will be removed and discarded before serving soup. Add enough water to cover prawns and three extra cups to make soup. Add the soy and sweet chili sauces and simmer for 15 minutes. Add the rice noodles, lettuce and cabbage slices and in 5 minutes the noodles should be ready. Turn off the heat and serve with lemon juice.

Main Meals

Aunt Despo's Mousaka

Ingredients:

- 1 kilogram eggplants
- 1 kilogram minced meat
- 1 large chopped onion
- 4 tablespoons dry breadcrumbs
- $^1/_2$ cup dry white wine
- 2 tablespoons chopped parsley
- 2 cloves garlic, crushed
- 2 tablespoons olive oil
- 500 grams peeled, chopped tomatoes
- 1 cup grated cheese
- 2 tablespoons tomato paste
- 1 teaspoon sugar
- Salt and pepper
- 1 egg

Method:

Cut eggplants into 5-millimeter slices, sprinkle with salt, and leave for 1 hour. Rinse and dry with paper towel; fry lightly in hot oil. Remove with a slotted spoon and place on paper towel to drain. Fry onion and garlic in oil until soft. Add minced meat, stir, and cook until brown. Add the tomatoes and tomato paste, salt, sugar, and pepper; bring to a boil. Simmer on low heat for 45 minutes until almost dry. Grease an oven dish and sprinkle with half the breadcrumbs. Add 1 layer of eggplant slices, top with half the meat sauce, and sprinkle with more crumbs and half the grated cheese. Repeat for a second layer. Pour béchamel sauce (recipe below) on top, sprinkle with extra cheese and bake at 180 degrees Celsius for 1 hour. Cool for 10 minutes, cut into squares, and serve. You can also add thin slices of potatoes with the eggplant slices.

Béchamel Sauce

Ingredients:

- 1 liter milk
- 90 grams plain flour
- 40 grams butter
- 2 eggs
- Salt and pepper for taste

Method:

Whisk together all ingredients in a pot over medium heat. Bring to the boil, stirring continuously with a whisk, until mixture thickens, and remove from heat.

Mom's Koubebia (Stuffed Grape Leaves)

Ingredients:

- $1^1/_2$ cups uncooked rice
- 1 cup boiling water
- 2 large onions, finely chopped
- $^1/_2$ cup olive oil and extra for frying
- 500 grams beef or pork minced meat
- 2 tablespoons mint or dill
- Salt and pepper
- 450 milliliters grape leaves, washed and drained
- Juice of 2 big lemons

Method:

Soak rice in boiling water for a half hour and drain. In a pot, fry the onion with some olive oil until transparent. Add the minced meat, mint, salt, pepper, and rice; mix until mince is a brown color. The rice does not have to be fully cooked. Leave to cool. Place a vine leaf on a board shiny side down and place a heaping teaspoon of filling toward the stem end. Roll once, fold in the sides, and roll up neatly. Place 5 or 6 leaves at the bottom of a saucepan, then pack the stuffed grape leaves on top, side by side, in layers. Add the lemon juice, 1 cup water, and $^1/_2$ cup olive oil. Place an inverted plate on top to stop rolls from opening, cover, and simmer over low heat for 45 minutes. Allow to cool in pan, remove carefully, and serve with yogurt.

Rena's Drunk Chicken

Ingredients:

- Sunflower oil for frying
- 3 large onions, finely chopped
- 3 cloves garlic, peeled and crushed
- 1 whole chicken, cut into pieces
- $1^1/_2$ teaspoons salt, pinch of pepper, and pinch of dry thyme
- 5 mushrooms, thickly sliced (optional)
- 2 cans of beer
- 10 baby potatoes, washed

Method:

Put a little oil in a deep, medium-sized nonstick pot, and, once it is hot, fry the onions until they are transparent. Add the garlic and the chicken pieces, and fry over medium heat until chicken skin turns a golden brown color. Lower the heat and add salt, pepper, thyme, and mushrooms. Pour in the 2 beers and add the baby potatoes on top of the chicken pieces. Partly cover the pot and simmer on low heat for about 1 hour until the potatoes are soft and the chicken is cooked. If the potatoes are ready before the chicken, remove them from the pot, so that they do not break. Keep an eye on the food - if the liquid evaporates, the food might burn on the bottom of the pot. Stir gently and add water if necessary. Transfer to a serving dish with its sauce and serve with bread for dipping

Desserts and cakes

Aunt Maria's Pavlova

Ingredients:

- 4 egg whites
- 250 milliliters/1 cup castor sugar
- 1 teaspoon corn flour
- 1 teaspoon white vinegar
- 1 teaspoon vanilla essence

Method:

Preheat oven to 180 degrees Celsius. Beat egg whites until white, fluffy, and soft-peak stage. Slowly add castor sugar until the whites form shiny, hard peaks. Add corn flour, vinegar, and vanilla essence; fold ingredients all together and shape into small rounds on to tray.

Bake for 2 hours at 100 degrees Celsius. Leave in oven until the meringues have cooled down. Serve with fresh cream, strawberries, kiwi fruit, banana, or any fruit of your liking.

Aunt Maria's Carrot Cake

Ingredients:

- $2\frac{1}{2}$ cups grated carrots
- $2\frac{1}{2}$ cups cake flour
- 1 cup chopped walnuts
- $1\frac{1}{2}$ cups sugar
- 4 eggs
- 1 teaspoon baking powder
- $1\frac{1}{4}$ cups sunflower oil
- $\frac{3}{4}$ teaspoon salt
- 2 teaspoons cinnamon
- 1 teaspoon bicarbonate of soda

Method:

Mix all ingredients together, place in a greased medium sized cake tin, and bake in oven at 180 degrees Celsius for about 40 minutes or until cake is ready.

Icing:

Mix together 100 grams butter with 250 grams cream cheese and 150 grams confectioner's sugar. Ice the cake once it has cooled.

....

Uncle Theo's Chocolate Cake

Ingredients:

- 4 eggs
- 1 cup sugar
- $\frac{1}{4}$ cup sunflower oil
- Pinch of salt
- $\frac{1}{4}$ cup cocoa powder
- 2 teaspoons baking powder
- 1 cup cake flour
- 1 teaspoon vanilla essence
- $\frac{1}{2}$ cup boiling water

Method:

Beat eggs and sugar very well with a mixer. Add oil and dry ingredients and mix. Add vanilla essence and water. Preheat oven to 180 degrees Celsius and bake in a medium sized cake pan for $1\frac{1}{2}$ hours or until cake is ready.

My Icing:

In a pot, boil some water, place a heat-resistant bowl on top, and melt together: 100 grams white cooking chocolate, 100 grams dark cooking chocolate, 1 tablespoon of butter, 1 drop of brandy, and 2 tablespoons of fresh cream. Ice the cake once it has cooled.

Dora's Cheesecake

Ingredients:

- 1 packet Tennis biscuits (or Digestive biscuits)
- 50 grams unsalted butter
- 250 grams cream cheese
- 1 can condensed milk
- $1/2$ cup lemon juice and a pinch of lemon grind
- 1 small packet gelatin
- 250 milliliters fresh cream
- Small can cherry pie filling

Method:

Crush biscuits in a blender, melt butter in microwave, pour over biscuits, and mix with a fork. Spread the biscuit mix on the bottom of a heat-resistant medium sized glass dish and place in a 180-degree Celsius oven for a few minutes until biscuits are golden brown. Remove and flatten biscuits with fork, making an even base; allow to cool. Using an electric mixer, mix together the cream cheese, condensed milk, fresh cream, lemon juice, lemon grind and gelatin, which has previously been dissolved in a tablespoon of hot water; pour mixture on top of biscuits, put in fridge for at least an hour, and then add the cherry filling on top. Keep in fridge until ready to serve.

Dora's Milk Tart

Ingredients:

- Tennis biscuits (or Digestive biscuits)
- 50 grams of margarine, melted
- 500 grams milk
- 25 grams flour
- 1 tablespoon corn flour
- 125 grams sugar
- 1 egg
- Vanilla essence
- Cinnamon powder to sprinkle on top

Method:

Crush biscuits in a blender, place in a small Pyrex dish, and mix with the melted margarine. Place in an oven at 180 degrees Celsius for 10 minutes or until biscuits are golden brown. Spread out in dish to make an even base. Whisk the rest of the ingredients in a pot; on medium heat, stirring continuously, bring to the boil and remove from heat. (Or, in Thermo-mixer, mix all ingredients at speed 4, 90 degrees, for 10 minutes.) Pour mixture in the Pyrex dish. Allow to cool and set and sprinkle the top with a pinch of cinnamon powder.

Angela's Vanilla Cupcakes
(Makes 12)

Ingredients:

- 100 grams butter
- 100 grams castor sugar
- 2 large eggs
- 100 grams self-raising flour
- 1 teaspoon baking powder
- Teaspoon vanilla essence (or vanilla powder)
- 10 milliliters boiling water
- 150 grams confectioner's sugar

Method:

Preheat oven to 190 degrees Celsius. Beat together butter and castor sugar until light. Add eggs and beat well. Add one teaspoon of vanilla essence and fold in flour and baking powder. Place cupcake paper liners into muffin tins. Spoon the mixture into liners. Bake in a preheated oven for 12-15 minutes or until they have risen and are a golden color. Remove and allow to cool.

Icing:

Sift confectioner's sugar in to a small bowl and stir in 10 milliliters boiling water and a drop of vanilla essence. Stir until smooth and ice the cakes once they have cooled down.

My Giant Peanut Butter Cookies
(Makes 10)

Ingredients:

- 60 grams butter, chopped
- $1/_2$ cup smooth peanut butter
- $1/_2$ cup castor sugar
- $1/_2$ cup brown sugar
- 1 egg, beaten
- 1 cup self-raising flour

Method:

Beat butter, peanut butter, and sugars in a deep bowl with an electric mixer until light and fluffy. Add egg and beat together. Stir in flour with spatula until well mixed. Roll handfuls of the mixture into balls. Place 5 centimeters apart on baking-paper-covered oven trays. Flatten mixture slightly. Bake in a preheated oven, 150 degrees Celsius for 15 minutes or until biscuits are a light brown color. Cool on trays.

Ero's Melomakarona (Christmas Biscuits)
(Makes 10)

Ingredients:

For biscuits:
- 2 cups oil
- $1/_2$ cup orange juice
- 1 cup sugar
- 1 teaspoon cinnamon
- $1/_2$ cup brandy
- $7 1/_2$ cups cake flour
- 2 teaspoons baking powder
- 1 teaspoon baking soda
- Grated walnuts

For the syrup
- 2 cups honey
- 2 cups sugar
- 2 cups water

Method:

Mix all biscuit ingredients together with a mixer. Using your fingers, make oval-shaped blobs and place on a greased baking tray; bake in a preheated oven at 180 degrees Celsius for 25 minutes. Bring all the syrup ingredients to the boil. Allow to cool. Once the biscuits are ready, dip them while still warm for a few minutes into a cooled syrup. Take them out and place on a serving dish. Sprinkle with a bit of additional honey and grated walnuts.

Mom's Vasilopita (New Year's Cake)

Ingredients:

- 4 cups plain white cake flour
- 5 tablespoons baking powder
- 2 cups sugar
- $1^1/_2$ cups milk
- 1 cup unsalted butter, melted
- 1 tablespoon grated rind of orange
- 3 eggs
- Icing sugar
- 1 coin wrapped in foil

Method:

Sift flour and baking powder; add sugar and place in mixing bowl. Add all other ingredients except eggs, icing sugar, and coin. Beat well on medium speed. Add eggs and continue beating for 2 minutes. Pour in a medium sized greased baking pan and bake at 180 degrees Celsius for 55 minutes. Sprinkle with icing sugar and serve on New Year's Day. Do not forget to insert a coin wrapped in foil, underneath the cake. Whoever finds the coin in his slice of cake will have good luck for the rest of the year.

Anna's Malva Pudding

Ingredients:

Batter:
- 20 grams butter, plus extra to grease baking dish
- 250 grams castor sugar
- 2 eggs
- 12.5 grams smooth apricot jam
- 5 grams bicarbonate of soda
- 125 grams milk
- 5 grams brown sugar
- 1 teaspoon brown vinegar

- 250 grams cake flour, sifted
- Pinch salt

Sauce:
- 250 grams cream
- 180 grams sugar
- 125 grams butter
- 125 grams boiling water
- 5 grams vanilla essence

Method:

Preheat oven to 180 degrees Celsius. Grease a medium sized ovenproof dish with butter. Cream together the butter and sugars. Add eggs one by one, beating well. Add jam. Blend bicarbonate of soda with the milk and add the vinegar. Add sifted flour and salt to the butter mixture, alternating with the milk. Spoon the batter into the prepared dish and bake in the preheated oven for 45 minutes, or until a testing skewer comes out clean when inserted into the center of the pudding.

Sauce:
Mix all the ingredients for the sauce and bring to the boil. Pour the hot sauce over the pudding as soon as it comes out of the oven. Serve with custard, vanilla ice cream, or whipped cream.

Demetra's South-African Koeksisters

Ingredients:

Syrup:
- 625 grams white sugar
- 250 grams water
- 15 grams lemon juice
- 5 grams vanilla essence, or a piece of bruised ginger

Dough:
- 375 grams cake flour
- 22 grams baking powder
- 1 grams salt
- 25 grams butter or margarine
- 150 grams milk
- 750 grams sunflower oil for deep frying

Method:

Syrup:
Bring the sugar and water to the boil in a deep saucepan, uncovered. Stir until sugar has dissolved. Simmer the syrup for 7 minutes, uncovered. (It must not become too thick.) Remove saucepan from the stove and stir in the lemon juice and vanilla essence. Chill in the fridge.

Dough:
Sift together the flour, baking powder, and salt. Rub in the butter and add the milk slowly, folding mixture with a spatula to form a dough. Cut 5 millimeter thick pieces. On a floured surface roll out dough pieces into narrow strips, to form long snake shapes, and plait the ends together. Heat the oil in a medium saucepan until hot (but not smoking hot). Put 3-4 koeksisters into the oil at a time and deep fry them first on one side, then on the other until they are a golden brown color. Remove the koeksisters with a slotted spoon and immediately plunge them into cold syrup. When the koeksisters are drenched with the syrup, remove them with a slotted spoon and transfer them to a wire rack set over a tray or dish. Serve them well chilled.

'You have succeeded in writing both a loving memoir and an engaging, entertaining tale—very well done. I can see the book being enjoyed as a window into another way of life and as an immigrant's tale. The recipes are a wonderful addition and will provide the reader with an even fuller experience.'

—Janet, Editor US

"ΜΟΛΙΣ ΕΧΩ ΔΙΑΒΑΣΕΙ ΤΟ ΒΙΒΛΙΟ ΣΟΥ ΕΛΕΝΑ. ΕΥΧΑΡΙΣΤΟΥΜΕ ΠΟΥ ΕΙΧΕΣ ΤΗΝ ΔΥΝΑΜΗ ΝΑ ΞΕΓΥΜΝΩΣΕΙΣ ΤΗΝ ΨΥΧΗ ΣΟΥ. ΕΜΕΙΣ ΔΥΣΚΟΛΕΥΟΜΑΣΤΕ ΝΑ ΤΟ ΚΑΝΟΥΜΕ ΑΚΟΜΑ ΚΑΙ ΣΤΟΝ ΨΥΧΟΛΟΓΟ!!! ΕΙΣΑΙ ΑΥΘΕΝΤΙΚΗ ΑΛΗΘΙΝΗ !!Ο ΘΕΟΣ ΝΑ ΣΕ ΕΧΕΙ ΚΑΛΑ!"

—Ariadne, Greek-Cypriot, Cyprus

"Elena has written a truly unique book. There are stories, and recipes, and heritage and ancestry, yet, it is also a travel book. She has captured remarkable moments and memories, and sights and tastes. This book is truly a delight for all your senses, and an absolute pleasure to read. The recipes are an added bonus like a little personal gift from the author after reading her story. It's fresh, and different, and makes you smile and makes you cringe too. And I loved it from the first to the last page. Highly recommended."

—Shahana, Brisbane, Australia